Treasure of Kalidasa Series 06

RAGHU VAMSHA
OR
AN ACCOUNT OF THE FAMILY OF RAGHU

Treasure of Kalidasa Series 06

RAGHU VAMSHA
OR
AN ACCOUNT OF THE FAMILY OF RAGHU

BY

KALIDASA

[TRANSLATED INTO ENGLISH PROSE.]

PUBLISHED BY
THE SOCIETY FOR THE RESUSCITATION
OF INDIAN LITERATURE.

GYAN

Published by

GYAN

Gyan Publishing House
5, Ansari Road
Daryaganj, New Delhi-110002
Phone: 011-47034999, 9811692060
E-mail: books@gyanbooks.com

Distribution Network
gyanbooks.com
India, USA, Canada, UK, Australia, France

ISBN : 978-81-212-24352 (PB)
First Published, 1901

2nd Impression 2021

Printed at: Gyan Press, Delhi.

Treasure of Kalidasa Series 06
Raghu Vamsha
or
An Account of the Family of Raghu
Translated by: Kalidasa

RAGHU VAMSHA

OR

AN ACCOUNT OF THE FAMILY OF RAGHU.

BY

KALIDASA.

[*TRANSLATED INTO ENGLISH PROSE.*]

PUBLISHED BY

THE SOCIETY FOR THE RESUSCITATION
OF INDIAN LITERATURE.

CALCUTTA:

PRINTED BY H. C. DAS, ELYSIUM PRESS,
Kashi Ghose's Lane, Beadon Street.

1901.

RAGHU VAMSHA

OR

AN ACCOUNT OF THE FAMILY OF RAGHU.

I wish to write about this family for many sages had done so before ; just as a thread may pass through parts bored with a diamond.

Though I am not rich in words yet I wish to write the history of the kings of Raghu's family who led pure lives from their birth, who were persevering in all their undertakings till they were successful, whose empires extended up to the Sea, whose cars went up to the celestial region, who duly offered oblations to the sacred fire, who gave to every one what he prayed for, who administered punishment to the offenders proportionate to their crimes, who always worked in proper hours, who amassed wealth only to be given to the poor, who spoke very little from the fear of deviating from the truth, who made wars only to acquire fame, who took wives only to beget children, who acquired learning in boyhood, who managed worldly affairs in youth, who retired into woods in old age, and who died engaged in religious meditation. Their accomplishments being present in my ears have induced me to undertake this bold work.

Those who can discriminate good and evil are qualified to read my work. It is fire alone that can testify the purity and impurity of gold.

In the days of yore there flourished a son of the sun by name Manu. He was respected of the learned. As Om is the first letter of the Vedas so he was the first progenitor of all kings.

As the moon originated from the ocean of milk so the pure-souled Dilipa was born in the pious family of Manu.

He had a broad chest and a bull-like neck. He was long-armed and tall like a *Sala* tree. He was as if the Kshatriya virtue incarnate on earth to do its duty.

He was like the lofty mount Meru extending over the earth excelling all in the hardness of its essence and brightness of its colour.

His wisdom was like his stature and his knowledge of Scriptures was like his intellect. His actions were in consonance with his knowledge of Shastras and his success was in keeping with his actions.

By his dreadful form and royal qualities he was unto his dependants like an ocean by its jems and aquatic animals.

As driven by an expert charioteer the after-wheel of a car does not transgress the track of the fore-wheel, so his subjects did not deviate from the moral laws observed since the time of Manu.

The sun draws moisture from the earth to pay her a thousand-fold in return. So did he collect tributes from his subjects for their well-being.

His army was like the umbrella, chowri and other parapharnalia of royalty. For achieving his end he depended upon his ability to understand Scripture properly and his skill in drawing his bow.

Like unto pristine impressions his actions, who was of close counsels, and whose gestures never betrayed his mind, were judged only by the result.

Fear never urged him on to defend himself, misfortune never made him pious, avarice did not tempt him to collect money, love of pleasure never prompted him to seek it.

He observed silence in a secret confided to him, forgave an offender even when able to punish him and never praised himself in good works. All these qualities were in him in unision.

He was not addicted to sexual pleasures, was a master of every department of knowledge and led a pious life. He had every advantage of old age without decrepitude.

He made arrangements for the education, maintenance and safety of his people. He was a father to them all, their own fathers giving them birth only.

He was learned. He married for the sake of children and punished the guilty for the behoof of his subjects. Thus virtue led him to acquire wealth and objects of enjoyment.

He milched the earth for performing sacrifices (for Indra) who in return milched the sky for his crops. Thus they governed both the worlds exchanging their good things.

No other king could acquire so much fame as he, for theft was entirely unknown in his territories, people knowing only the term.

An honourable enemy was to him like medicine to a patient. But he could cast a friend, proved bad, as a finger bit by a serpent.

Forsooth God created him with the ingredients of five elements for like them his qualities were employed for the good of others.

The sea-coast was the wall and the ocean itself the entrenchment of his empire. There was no other ruler of the earth and he governed it like his own household. He had a wife by name Sudakshina born in the family of Magadha. As becoming her name she was kind and benevolent. She was to the king what *Dakshina* is to sacrifice.

Though he had other wives he considered Sudakshina and Lakshmi as his true wives.

He was anxious to have a son by his favourite consort Sudakshina and was impatient to see the day when his desire would be satisfied.

In order to perform certain ceremonies for begetting a son he handed over the administration to his minister.

Having worshipped Brahma the self-controlled pair set out for the hermitage of their preceptor Vasistha with a view to have a son.

They went on a car making a soft and deep sound and looked like lightning and Airavata riding the clouds of the rainy season.

To avoid disturbing the hermitage they took a few retainers with them. But their natural dignity inspired the on-lookers with such an awe as if they had an army with them.

Gently shaking the forest trees and carrying the fragrance of sal and filaments of flowers pleasant breeze comforted them on the way.

Mistaking the deep rattle of the car-wheel for the rumbling of clouds the peacock and pea-hen emitted sweet notes. And the cries of the male and female birds, resembling the first note of the music, delighted their ears.

The male and female deer gazed on the passing car and the king and queen, as they passed on, compared their eyes with theirs.

Sometimes they cast their looks upwards on rows of cranes emitting sweet notes and resembling garlands suspended on gates without any support.

As if fore-boding the fulfillment of their object auspicious wind blew from behind so that the dust raised by the horse's hoof could not touch the crown of the king or the curling locks of the queen.

They smelt the sweet odour of the full blown lotus resembling their own breath in fragrance, which was cooled by the contact of the waves of the lake.

As they passed through villages gifted away by them in which there were pillars commemorating the same they received offerings of honour and blessings from the Brahmanas who were in possession thereof.

They met with milkmen carrying fresh butter and asked them to describe the names of the wild trees that had grown on the road side.

Thus while putting on pure dress and both seated on the same seat the king with his queen went on they looked beautiful like the moon of pure rays emerging from midst with the planet Chitra by his side.

The learned and the beautiful king was busy in pointing various objects on the road side to his wife so that he could not perceive the distance they had traversed.

He, of renown hard to acquire, and whose horses were fatigued, reached, along with his queen, the hermitage of the great self-controlled Rishi in the evening.

It was being filled with ascetics returned from woods, with fuel, flowers and fruits and welcomed by fire invisible to ordinary observers.

There the deer, accustomed to feed on *niba* rice,

given them by the female anchorites, obstructed the doors as if they were their children.

There having watered the plants the ascetic girls went away in great haste lest they might frighten birds come for drinking the water.

In the yards of the hermitages in the evening grass and paddy dried by the sun were collected in heaps and the deer lay down at ease and chewed the cud.

There smoke, fragrant with the perfume of burnt offerings and indicating a burning fire raised by the wind, purified the hearts of guests coming to that sacred place.

Having ordered the charioteer to look after the horses the king helped the queen to descend and then himself got down from the car.

The polite ascetics, whose senses had been controlled, received with due honor their wise protector, the king and his royal wife.

The king saw the ascetic Vasistha who had just finished his evening rites, seated on the same seat with his wife Arundhuti. They looked like Agni and his wife Swaha seated side by side.

The king and the queen, the princess of Magadha saluted the preceptor and his wife; they too welcomed them with blessings.

After offering them the rites of hospitality and removing their exhaustion the ascetic enquired about the welfare of his kingdom.

Then the King, the best of speakers and the conqueror of enemy's cities, addressed Vasistha, who was well versed in the Astharva Veda, in words fraught with noble sense.

"While thou art my protector against calamities caused by men and gods it is certain that every thing is well in my seven members.

Thy mystic formulæ subdue unseen foes whereas my arrows pierce visible objects only. So by the power of thy mantras my arrows have been made useless.

The offerings, thrown by thee duly into the sacred fire, are converted into rain and revive the withered crops of my empire.

It is owing to thy Brahminic influence my subjects live long, spend their days fearlessly and are never visited by calamities of drought and excessive rain.

When my spiritual guide, Brahma's son, is anxious on my account, what wonder is that I am secure from dangers and shall enjoy perpetual happiness.

But as I have got no children by this thy daughter-in-law, the world, with all the islands, although abounding in many precious things, cannot conduce to my happiness.

My departed manes cannot enjoy to their full satisfaction the offerings I present to them at the Sraddha but keep a portion of them in reserve fearing that such offerings will terminate after my death.

They drink the oblations of water, offered by me,

heated with their sighs thinking that they shall no longer have them after my death.

By celebrating sacrifices I have paid my debts to the celestials, but having so sons I have not been able to satisfy my debts to my ancestral manes. I am like the Lokaloka mountain, half lighted by the Sun and half enshrouded in darkness.

The fruits of devotion and charity make as happy in the after life but children of good lineage conduce to happiness both here and hereafter.

Dost thou not feel as much pain on seeing me childless as thou experiencest on finding the tree of the asylum, carefully reared by thy own hands, bearing no fruits ?

My debt to my departed manes pains me as much as the stake does a newly caught elephant tied to it.

O Father, do for me that by which I may satisfy that debt. Thou art alone able to gratify the wishes of the Ikshwakus when they themselves fail to do so."

Hearing the king's prayer Vasistha engaged in meditation with closed eyes for some time and remained as calm as a lake undisturbed by fishes. By the power of concentration the self-controlled (Rishi) could find out what stood in the way of the king's getting a son and said.

"O king, once on a time in the days of yore, while you were returning to earth after having served the king of celestials the worshipful cow Surabhi was lying down on the road side under the shade of the desire-fulfilling tree. Fearing lest you might fail in your duty by Sudakshina who had just bathed after menses, you forgot to pay her due honors.

She imprecated therefore a curse on you, saying "For thus dishonoring me you will not got a son till you worship my child."

Owing to the noise of the waters of the etherial Ganges disturbed by the sportive elephants of the quarters neither yourself nor your charioter could hear the curse.

For thus dishonoring the cow your heart's desire has not been fulfilled for our welfare is injured when we fail to honor them to whom honor is due.

Guarded by serpents she is now in the nether world for giving butter and milk to the regent of water, necessary for the celebration of a sacrifice in which he is engaged.

Being purified, yourself and your queen worship her child and representative Nandini; when she will be propitiated your desire will be crowned with success."

While Vasistha was giving him this advice the fault-less cow Nandini, which enabled him to feed the sacred fire, returned from the forest.

She was of the reddish colour like a new leaf and there was a white curve line on her fore-head. She resembled evening crowned with the crescent.

As she saw her calf she sprinkled the earth with lukewarm milk, holier than the sacred ablution, from her plump teats.

The dust raised by her feet covered the king's body who stood hard by and sanctified it as if he had bathed in the sacred stream. The ascetic, conversant with the prognostications of good and evil; seeing the holy Nandini approach the hermitage, said to the king whose desire was about to be fulfilled.

" O king, when the blessed Nandini has just arrived with the mention of her name the time is not far off when your object will be accom plished.

Living on roots and fruits you should propitiate her by constantly following her as one should please the goddess of learning by study.

You should walk when she walks, stand when she stands, and sit and drink when she does so.

My daughter-in-law too, being self-controlled, should follow her reverentially to the end of the hermitage in the morning and advance thither in the evening to receive her.

Thus serve her till she is pleased. May no mishap stand in your way and may you be the happiest of fathers as your father was on obtaining you as his son."

The disciple, conversant with the knowledge of time and place, along with his wife, accepted the command of their preceptor by bending low their heads and saying " So be it."

The night approaching the truthful and polite Vasistha, the son of Brahma, asked the king, whose happiness was about to down, to retire.

Vasistha, conversant with the knowledge of ceremonies, gave him fruits, roots and a bed of straw in consideration of what he was to perform, though he could procure him all the things of the world through his power of devotion.

In pursuance of the set rules the royal pair passed the night on the straw bed given them by that prince of hermits and rose in the morning hearing Vasistha's disciples chant the Vedas.

CANTO II.

In the morning after the queen had presented to Rishi's cow perfume and garlands and after the calf had been tied after milking, the king, having glory for his wealth, set her free for going to the forest.

Like Smriti following the Sruti, the queen, the foremost of the chaste women, followed closely the track of the cow, sanctified by the dust of her hoofs.

Having sent back his queen to the hermitage the illustrious and the kind-hearted king began to protect Nandini who could give more milk than the water of the four oceans and who resembled the earth in the shape of a cow having four seas for four teats.

For celebrating the vow he sent away his remaining followers though they wanted to follow him. He stood in need of no external help for his protection for the descendants of Vaivaswata could protect themselves by their own prowess.

The king tended the cow by collecting sweet grass, brushing his body, driving away flies and permitting her to graze at large.

He stopped when the cow stopped, walked when she walked, stood up when she stood up and drank when she drank. He followed her as her own shadow.

Though there was no insignia of royalty on his person still he had such an effulgence that people could know him as a king. He was like an young elephant full of native wildness not yet sufficiently known.

While traversing the forest ways the trees on both the sides, with the sweet notes of the birds, used to sing the glories of the Varuna-like energetic king who had no followers by him.

When that king, effulgent like the fire, used to approach the creepers, they, shaken by the breeze, dropped flowers on him, like women of the city who used to welcome him with a downpour of fried grain.

The native mildness of his nature shining through his countenance begat so much confidence in the female deer, that though he had a bow in hand they used to gratify their large eyes by gazing at him without any fear.

He heard the presiding gooddess of the forest sing aloud his praise while the wind, passing through the holes in the bamboos, made a music similar to that of the flutes.

Cooled by the water of the mountain-spring, carrying the perfume of the gently shaken flowers the wind refreshed the pious king who was without any umbrella and therefore stricken with heat.

When he entered the woods, the forest fire was put out without rain; fruits and flowers grew in profusion and stronger animals did not prey on the weaker.

In the evening the sun, red as the new leaves, and the hermit's cow used to walk homeward sanctifying the quarters.

The King followed Nandini who used to help the ascetic in worshipping the gods, in performing annual Sraddhas of his ancestors and in treating his his guests. Followed by Dilipa, adored of the sages, she shone like faith followed by action. As he went on he saw the woodland strewn with swine just risen from muddy pools, the peacocks going to their sheltering trees and flocks of antelopes lying on the grass.

Being pained by the weight of her udders the cow, that had given birth to one calf only, went on slowly. The king too, on account of the heaviness of her person, went on slowly. Their view was indeed very charming.

Nandini, followed by the king, and welcomed by

the queen by coming in advance looked like twilight between day and night.

Having circumambulated and bowed to her with a vessel of offerings in her hand Sudakshina respectfully poured them on the part of her head intervening between her two beautiful horns, which was like the gate of success.

Although impatient to see her calf yet Nandini stood still and accepted the offerings. The king and the queen were really pleased to see this, for signs of gratification displayed by great men indicate the fullfilment of the object of their proteges.

Having prostrated himself at the feet of his spiritual guide and his wife and performed the evening rites, Dilipa again began to serve the calf of Suravi lying at ease after being milked.

The royal pair put offerings and a light near Nandini, they slept after she had fallen asleep and got up in the morning as soon as she was awake.

Thus observing the vow for a son, the king, who was well known for relieving the poor of their sufferings, passed twenty-one days along with his queen.

On the twenty-second day being desirous of testing the sincerity of her follower, the asceti's cow entered into a grassy cave of the Himalaya near the falls of the Ganges.

Knowing well that beasts of prey would never think of attacking her far from doing it actually the unsuspecting king feasted on the grandeur of the mountain when suddenly a lion sprang on her.

The cries of the cow, growing louder by the echoe, drew, as it were by the pulling of reins, the eyes of the king, the helper of the distressed, fixed on the mountain.

Then the king, with bow in hand, saw the reddish yellow cow with a long mained lion on her like the blossoming Lodhra tree growing on the mountain side filled with red earth.

Considering himself insulted the king, quick-coursing like a lion, the refuge of those seeking shelter, and the conqueror of the enemy's city, took out an arrow from his quiver to kill the lion that richly deserved to be killed.

As being anxious to kill the lion he was about to take up the arrow the fingers of his right hand remained fixed on the feather, as if in a picture, beautifying his nails.

His right hand being thus rendered immoveable and incapable of punishing the offender he raged like a serpent rendered inert by drugs and incantations.

The king, who was lion-like in prowess and a friend of the pious, was surprised on seeing his limbs paralysed. It was intensified, when the lion, that caught the cow, began to speak like a human being.

"O king, useless is thy attempt. Even if thou couldst discharge thy weapons they would prove futile. The force of the wind can uproot trees but it cannot stand before the mountain.

I am the servant of Siva. He sanctifies my back by placing his feet on it whenever he rides his bull white like the mount Kailasha. My name is Kumbhodara and I am a friend of Nikumbha.

Look at the yo fire tree. It has been adopted by the bull-ensigned Siva as his son. It has been nursed by Skanda's mother by pouring water from golden pots.

One day a wild elephant tore its bark by rubbing his cheek against it. Thereat the Himalay's daughter was as much stricken with grief as she was when she saw Kartika wounded by the arrows of the Asuras.

Since then the trident-handed deity has appointed me a guard to drive away the elephants; and at his behest I live upon animals that approach this spot.

Mahadeva has been pleased to send this cow at the hour when I take my food. Her blood shall satisfy me as the moon's ambrosia gratifies Rahoo.

Thou art helpless. Desist casting off shame. Thou hast shown sufficient devotion to thy preceptor as a disciple. The reputration of a warrior does not suffer the least if he cannot, by the use of his weapons, save the object he seeks to protect."

Hearing these prouds words of the lion the King was convinced that his weapon was nullified by the power of the lord of Kailasha and therefore his contempt towards himself was decreased.

As Indra, while he was about to hurl his thunderbolt, was stupified by the glances of Virupaksha, so was the king who for the first time failed to discharge the weapon. He answered the lion saying."

" O king of animals, while my attempt to kill you has become futile, surely what I will say will create redicule. But as thou canst go through the hearts of men I shall do so.

I submit to the command of Mahadeva the creator, preserver and destroyer of all living and inanimats objects. But I cannot neglect this precious cow of my preceptor that is about to be killed before me.

Please therefore feast on my flesh and release my preceptor's cow. As the day is disappearing her calf is impatient to see her."

Smiling a little and lighting up the cave with the brightness of his teeth, the lion said :—

"O King, you are indiscreet enough in wishing to sacrifice the sovereignty of the world, youth and beautiful body for such an insignificant object.

It is true you have compassion for all living creatures—but consider your death will benefit this cow only whereas your life will protect your subjects against constant danger.

Your fear that your preceptor will be worked with anger like fire at the loss of his only cow; but you may appease his anger by presenting him with crores of cows with large udders.

Protect your strong and youthful body used to many luxuries. Your empire is like that of Indra, the only difference being that it is situate on earth."

When the king of animals stopped after saying this the mountain too, with the echo in his cave, said the same thing to the king.

Hearing the words of the lion, the follower of the god, and being looked at with pitiable eyes by the cow under his clutches the kind-hearted king again said.

"The great word Kshatra is universally known to signify *one who saves from danger*. If I act against that tradition of what use is a kingdom or a contaminated life to me?

O lion, how can I pacify the rage of the ascetic by presenting him with other cows in the place of Nandini who is not different from Surabhi. You have been able to attack her only by the power of Rudra.

It is my duty therefore to release her even at the cost of life. It will appease your hunger and the Homa ceremony of the ascetic will not be stopped.

You are devoted to your master. It is proved by your care of this fir tree. You know therefore a servant cannot appear before his master, without himself being wounded and losing the object of his care.

If you think that you should not kill me then spare my body of reputation instead of my corporeal frame. I consider this body of five elements as useless.

The wise say that conversation begets friendship. I have seen you in this forest and already a friendship has sprung up on account of the conversation. O servant of the lord of goblins, you should not disregard the request of a friend."

When the lion accepted his proposal by saying 'So be it' the king threw drown his arms and contracting his body presented a lump of flesh to the lion to be devoured by him.

As the king sat on the ground with his face bent down, looking at intervals towards the lion and expecting that it would jump on his shoulders the celestials showered flowers on him.

Then hearing the nectarine words "Rise up my son." the king stood up and saw that there was no lion. Filled with affection like his own mother the cow stood before him and milk flowed from her udders.

The cow said to the king, who was filled with surprise ;—"It is an illusion spread by me for testing your sincerety. What to speak of other animals even Yama, for the influence of the Rishi, cannot assail me.

Son, I am pleased to see your devotion to your preceptor and your compassion for me. Pray for a boon from me. Do not think me a cow that gives milk only. I can gratify people's wishes also when I am pleased."

Thus commanded, the king who granted the prayer of the supplicants, and who by the strength of his arms, had attained to the dignity of a heroe, with folded hands, prayed for a son, the perpetuator of his race, by his wife Sudakshina.

Having granted the boon of the king who was anxious to have a son the cow said :—"O son, hold my milk in a vessel of leaves and drink it."

The king replied :—" Mother, after your calf had drunk the milk and a portion had been reserved for Homa then with the permission of the Rishi, I will drink the remnant like the sixth part of the produce of the earth."

More pleased at these words than she had been before the cow proceeded happily from the mouun-tain cave towards the hermitage, the king follow-ing her.

Marking signs of joy on the king's face bright as the clear moon Vasistha and the queen inferred that Nandini had been pleased. So the king's narration of the subject was a mere repetition.

After Nandini's calf had drunk her milk and a portion had been reserved for Homa, the king, with his preceptor's permission, drank the remnant eagerly which was white and the very personification of fame.

With the termination of the vow the self-restrained

Vasistha blessed the royal pair in the following morning and permitted them to return to their capital.

Having circumambulated in order the sacred fire, Vasistha and his wife Arundhati and the cow with the calf by her side, the king left the hermitage with an air of dignity increased by the performance of auspicious ceremonies.

The king, ever untiring in his labour, with his religiously wedded wife, got upon his car which was like that of his own wishes and which being driven along an easy path, produced a sweet noise.

Gladdened at his return after a long absence his subjects repeatedly looked at the king, emaciated by the observance of a vow for getting a son but were not satiated for he was like the new moon to them after the expiration of the dark fortnight.

The king entered the capital, decorated with flags, amidst the çheers of the citizens, and took upon himself the burden af the world like the king of serpents.

As the damsels of the quarters held the lunar disc coming out of the eyes of the sage Atri, as the celestial stream Ganga held the semen of Siva discharged by the Fire-God so the queen Sudakshina conceived a child destined to perpetuate the Ikshaku race which was endued with the effulgence of the eight guardians deities of the quarters.

CANTO III.

Thereupon the Queen Sudakshina bore signs of pregnancy which was like her husband's desire about to fructify and a moon to her companions and indicated the continuity of the Ikshwaka family.

Being emaciated she could not decorate her person with ornaments and her complexion was pale like the Lodhra flower. She was like night verging on the dawn with a pale moon and a few stars.

As an elephant is not satiated with smelling the earthy scent of the new water of the pool in the forest soaked with rain at the termination of the summer so the king was not satiated with the earthy fragrance of her mouth when he met her in private.

The queen did not like any food except earth, perhaps because her son would be the sole ruler of the world as Indra is of the celestial region.

Dilipa, the king of North Kosala, used always to enquire kindly of the maids of the queen, saying "the princess of Magadha cannot out of shame ask for any thing she wishes to have. Can you tell me what she likes."

No sooner Sudakshina, stricken with a desire for articles of food but never relishing them, asked for any thing than, she was immediately supplied with them.

When her misery consequent on distaste was gone queen Sudakshina regained her health and looked beautiful like a creeper that, after leaving off old, leaves, has put forth new ones of greater beauty.

Owing to her nipples becoming dark in time, her large breasts excelled in beauty the full grown lotus buds with black-bees sitting on them.

The pregnant queen appeared to the eyes of the king like the earth abounding in jems, the Sami tree with fire lying inside and the Saraswati flowing through sand.

The king Dilipa performed *Punsavana* and other rites necessary for the pregnancy with grandeur proportionate to his love for her, to the wealth collected by the strength of his arms from the various quarters and the joy he experienced in expectation of a son.

Whenever the king went to her quarters the queen Sudakshina, having fickle eyes, rose up with difficulty from her seat in consequence of the weight of her womb containing the parts of the various presiding deities of the quarters and welcomed him with hands languidly joined together. This sight gave him great pleasure.

Trustworthy physicians, expert in the treatment of infants, nourished the embryo with great care and as the time of delivery was drawing nigh the queen appeared to her husband as the clouded welkin about to pour down showers.

As the energy manifesting itself in three forms, namely power, good counsel and readiness, gives birth to inexhaustible riches, so Sudakshina, like unto

Sachi herself, gave birth to a son in due time. Five of the planets were in ascendant and at a distance from the sun at the time and this indicated his future greatness.

At the time of the prince's birth the sky was clear, a delightful breeze was blowing, and the sacrificial fire, with its flame directed towards the south, received offerings of clarified butter. In fact every thing indicated good for the birth of such a man is intended for the behoof of the world.

The lying-in-room being lighted up on all sides with natural effulgance of the boy of auspicious birth the feeble mid-night lamps were put into shade and appeared like painted pictures.

Except the white um brella, bright as the rays of the moon and the two chowries the king gave away all his valuables to his attendant of the seraglio who conveyed to him the nectarine intelligence of the son's birth.

When the king saw the lovely face of his son with eyes motionless like the lotus in a lake where there is no wind his heart overflowed with delight like ocean on seeing the moon. The family priest Vasistha came from his hermitage and celebrated the birth-rites of Dilipa's son who shone like a diamond after it has been cleaned.

The birth-ceremony of the child was solemnized by the sweet music and dance of the courtezan's in the king's palace and also by the sound of Dundhavi in the celestial region.

No one had been in prison in the kingdom of Dilipa, a great and skilful adminstrator so on this occasion he had none to set at liberty except his own-self whom he released from the fetters of indebtedness to his departed manes.

Knowing that this boy would go to the other end of the ocean of scriptures and enemies, the king Dilipa, who was a master of roots of verbs, gave him the name of Raghu which is derived from the verb *lagh* meaning to go.

Under the fostering care of his immensely rich sire the prince Raghu grew up, as the moon, parmeated by the rays of the sun, increases in size after the period of conjunction.

Like unto Parvati and Mahadeva on the birth of the six-headed deity, like unto Sachi and Purandara on that of Jayanta, the queen Sudakshina and Dilipa who were like Uma and her husband, or Sachi and her lord, experienced great joy on obtaining a son equal to Kumara or Jayanta.

The mutual love of the royal pair like that of a couple of Chakravakas was increased rather than decreased on being shared by their only child.

Great was the delight of Dilipa when the nurse, taught the child to walk with the help of her fingers and bow down imitating her.

When the king placed him on his lap, the pleasure

caused by the the touch of his person, poured nectar on his body. With closed eyes he used to enjoyt that fong-sought-for pleasure.

As Brahma, the Creator of the world, regarded it stable through Vishnu, in whom the quality of Sattwa or goodness predominated, and who was but his another form, so the king, the protector of the world, regarded the perpetuity of his race secure through his son of most excellent birth.

After the celebration of his *Chuda* ceremony, the princes, along with the minister's sons of the same age, having flowing locks, entered into the ocean of words through his acquaintance with the fifty lettered alphabet.

In due time he was invested with sacrificial thread and placed under the tuition of learned teachers whose labors were crowned with success for instructions given to a worthy pupil always yeild fruits.

As the sun, by means of a horse swifter than the wind, rides from one end of the welkin to the other so Raghu, greatly endowed with intellectual powers, crossed the four oceans of knowledge.

Gradually going beyond boy-hood Raghu arrived at youth. And like the calf changed into a bull and the young of an elephant into a powerful animal his person displayed a beauty shorn of the fickleness of the boy-hood.

Dilipa then made him perform the rite of the cutting of the hair and had him married. The princesses bound to Ragh in the wedlock chain, appeared beautiful like the daughters of Daksha when united with the moon.

The arms of the highly powerful and the youthful Raghu were long like yokes, his breast was spacious like a door cover and his neck was thick. Though he surpassed his old father in size still he looked small by his humility.

At length desirous of lighting the heavy burden of governing the subjects which he had so long borne king Dilipa, who was gentle by nature and culture, installed Raghu as the heir-apparent of the throne.

As beauty gradually passes from a fading lotus to a new one, so the goddess of empire, appreciating merit, moved by degrees, from her principal residence the king Dilipa, to her new seat, lying nigh, the crown prince. Like the fire aided by the wind, like the sun in the autumn, like an elephant by the temporal juice the power of Dilipa became formidable by the help of his son Raghu.

Like the king of gods Dilipa celebrated ninety-nine horse sacrifices without any obstrution Raghu, with bow in hand, and his companions, guarded the sacrificial horse.

At last Indrà, in his invisible form, pilfered the horse, even before the very eyes of its guards armed with bows, let loose by Dilipa to wander at ease.

Raghu's soldiers were surprised at this sudden incident and knew not what to do. Just in the nick of time, Vasistha's cow, Nandini, of whose power the prince Raghu had heard before, came there roving at large.

Having washed his eyes with the sacred urine of Nandini, Dilipa's son, honored of the good, began to see objects beyond the ken of the senses.

The Prince espied Purandara, the cutter of the wings of mountains, fly eastward, with sacrificial horse tied to the car with a rope and repeatedly struck by the charioteer into quietness.

By his thousand winkless eyes and green horse he took him for Indra; and impeding him in the way he said, his voice touching the sky.

"O King of gods, the wise assign to thee the first place amongst the partakers of sacrificial offerings. Why dost thou obstruct the celebration of a sacrifice undertaken by my father who is always engaged in such sacrifices?

Thou art the lord of the three worlds and canst see objects imperciptible to the senses. It is proper for thee to punish them who hinder the celebration of sacrifices. If thou thyself standst in the way of good men performing good works there will be an end of it ere long.

Therefore, O Maghavan, thou shouldst return the horse which is the *sine quanon* of the sacrifice. Those who point out good ways never wend evil ways."

Hearing those bold words of Raghu the king of the celestials stopped his car and said.

"O Kshatrya boy, what you have said is true. But those who value fame should protect it from their enemies. Your father is about to excell my world-wide reputation by sacrifices.

The word "Purusottama or the best of male beings" designates Vishnu only; the word Maheswara or Great God" signifies the three-eyed Mahadeva only; similarly by the expression "the performer of a hundred sacrefices" the ascetics know me. All these three words have only one signification and not two.

Following in the wake of Kapila I have siezed this horse. Trying in vain to release do not attain yourself to the condition of the offspring of Sagara."

Again, Raghu, the guard of the sacrificial horse, spoke fearlessly to Purandara :—"If this is your firm resolve, take up your weapons. Know, you cannot achieve your end so long Raghu remains unconquered."

Saying this he raised up his head to set an arrow to his bow. He slightly advanced his right foot and threw back his left looking like Siva while he attempted to burn the celestial city of the Asura Tripura.

Waxing wroth at the hostile attitude of Raghu Indra set an inffallible shaft to his bow which is seen for a short time on the new clouds.

The arrow, which was ever used to drink the blood of the dreadful Asuras, pierced the broad chest of Dilip's son and began to drink human blood never tasted by it before.

The prince, who was like unto Kumara in prowess, shot an arrow with his own name engraven on it at the arm of Indra whose palm was hardened by goading the celestial elephant Airavata and was dyed with the paintings on Sachi's cheeks.

With a peacock-feathered arrow Raghu struck down the top of Indra's car with the figure of a thunder-bolt placed on it. At this the king of celestials was so much worked up with anger as if the hairs of the celestial goddess of fortune had been forcibly plucked.

There tock place a terrible encounter between the two warriors, each hoping for victory. Innumerable, dreadful feathered arrows went up and down. Filled with surprise the Siddhas stood by Indra and the troops of Raghu by him.

As with rain water a cloud cannot extinguish the fire of lightning begotten by itself so Indra could not defeat Raghu who had a portion of his unbearable essence in him.

Then Raghu shot a crescent shaped arrow, which soundig deep like the churning of the ocean, cut off the string of the bow held by Indra in his hand besmeared with scented sandal.

Burning in anger Indra cast off his bow and

bent upon killing his powerful enemy took up his burning thunder that had clipped off the wings of the mountains.

Struck at the breast by that powerful weapon Raghu dropped down on the ground along with the tears of his soldiers and recovering in a moment he rose up in the midst of their joyous exclamations.

Seeing Raghu unscathed even by that ruthless weapon the destroyer of Vitra was highly pleased with his great power for merit is honored everywhere.

Then Vasava spoke distinctly :—"This weapon of mine, well tempered, is invincible even when discharged againt the mountains. None but you has been able to withstand it. I am pleased with you. Tell me what you wish to have except this horse."

The Prince Raghu put into his quiver the half-raised arrow feathered in gold which had lightened his fingers and gently said to the king of the celestials.

"O lord, if thou art not willing to part with this horse do that by which my father, always engaged in the celebration of sacrifices, may reap the fruits of a fully performed horse sacrifice.

Holding an imperial assemblage for the horse sacrifice my father has assumed one of the forms of the eight-formed Siva and is therefore inaccessible to the common people. Send one of thy messengers to communicate to that best of kings what has happened.

Indra, having Matali for his charioteer, granted Raghu's prayer saying ' So be it" and drove towards his heavenly mansion. Raghu, with an indifferent heart, returned to the imperial assemblage.

Before his return to the palace king Dilipa had learnt every thing from Indra's emissary. So he received his son by touching his body, which bore the wound inflicted by the thunderbolt, with his hand, cooled with joy.

Desirous of having a station in the celestial region, thus did the king Dilipa perform in his old age ninety-nine horse-sacrifices which were as it were the so many steps for ascending the heaven.

In pursuance of the practice of the kings of the Ikshaku dynasty, who in old age retired from the world and engaged in meditative contemplation, the king, giving up all desires for worldly objects, made over duly the royal umbrella to his son, and adopted the *Vanaprastha* life along with his queen.

CANTO IV.

After the termination of the day, as the fire shines more brilliantly on receiving the light of the sun so acquiring the kingdom given by his Sire Raghu became more powerful than before.

On hearing of the establishment of Raghu on the throne of Dilipa the fire of grief that had been smoking in the hearts of conquered kings became as if ablaze.

As men eagerly look up to the rain-flag hoisted over the gate of a palace so the subjects of Raghu and their children were filled up with joy on seeing his elevation.

Raghu, of elephantine gait, simultaneously occupied his father's throne and his enemies' territories.

Hiding herself Lakshmi (the goddess of fortune) served the newly installed Raghu with her umbrella of the hundred petalled lotus.

Permeating the bodies of the panegyrists at the time of their singing his glories, the goddess of learning served that king, worthy of being lauded, with encomiums pregnant with meaning.

Though the earth had been enjoyed before by the adorable Manu and other kings yet she served Raghu devotedly like a wife who had no other husband.

By meting out punishment proportionate to the crimes he pleased his subjects like the south wind, neither too hot nor too cold.

As the fruits of the mangoe tree do not lead men to grieve for the flowers, so Raghu, by the excess of qualities, gave no occasion to his people to feel the loss of his sire.

Ministers, well versed in polity, pointed out to him what is good and what is bad and he adopted the former and discarded the latter.

On Raghu's accession to the throne, the five elements, earth etc, were greatly improved in quality so that every thing in his regeme appeared new.

As the appellation *chandra* of the moon is true for its giving delight and the name *Tapan* of the sun is so for imparting heat so Raghu made immense justice to his appellation *Raja* for he pleased his subjects.

True it is that he had eyes extending to the ears, but properly speaking his eyes were the Shastras by which he could see even the minutest duties. When Raghu was comfortable after establishing peace all through his kingdom, the autumn, having the lotus for its ensign, appeared before like the goddess of empire.

The light of the sun, whose course was unobstructed on account of the termination of the rain and the lightness of the clouds, and the irrepressible power of Raghu spread all over the quarters.

Indra, the king of the celestials, laid aside his rain-bow and Raghu took up his bow of victory. Thus the two, one after another, took up their respective bows, for the behoof of their subjects.

Having the lotus as if for his umbrella and the blossoming Kasa flowers for his chowries the autumn resembled Raghu but he could never equal the king in splendour.

With his gracious face the king and with pure rays, the moon, equally delighted the eyes of the spectators.

The brightness of Raghu's fame reflected itself in the flocks of geese, in the stars and in the water adorned with lilies. The wives of husbandmen, who guarded the corn-fields, sat in the shade of sugarcane plants and sang the glory of Raghu, begotten by his accomplishments, beginning with the incidents of his youth.

With the rising on one hand, of the very powerful Agastya (the star canopus) water became clean, and with Raghu's accession on the other hand to the throne, the hearts of his enemies became muddy with the fear of defeat.

Excited with the exhurberance of their strength humped bulls digged up the banks of rivers and thus imitated the prowess of Raghu.

Smelling the intoxicating odour of *Saptaparna* flowers the elephants exuded temporal juice, as if in emulation, from seven different parts of their bodies.

Making rivers fordable and drying up roads, the autumn urged on Raghu to set out for conquest before he was excited by the love of enterprise to do so.

The fire, lighted on the holy occasion of consecrating war-horses and fed duly with offerings, directing its flame towards the south, granted him victory as it were with its own hand.

Having made arrangements for defending his capital and out-lying forts against any foreign invasion, safe-guarding his army from any attack from behind and seeing favourable omens the king set out for conquest with six-fold forces.

As the drops of water, thrown up by the waves of the milk-ocean caused by the dashing of the churning rod, the mount Mandara, sprinkled the person of Vishnu so the aged ladies of the capital poured handfuls of fried grain on the person of the king when he started on the expedition of conquest.

The king, who was like unto Indra, first started towards the East with his flag shaken by the favourable wind, which as it were frowned upon his enemies.

The dust, raised the car-wheels and elephants by resembling so many clouds made the sky look like the earth, and the earth like the clouded sky.

First went his prowess, then the noise of his soldiers, then clouds of dust and last of all his four-fold forces. Thus, as if divided into four divisions, the army of Raghu marched on.

The king Raghu, of vast resources as he was, dug tanks in waterless tracts, bridged the navigable rivers and felled down the trees of the forest.

Commanding his own army the king shone like Bhagiratha taking the Ganga out of the matted locks of Hara and leading her to the East.

As the huge-tusked elephants went on uprooting the trees that fell in their way or breaking their branches or spoiling their fruits and flowers so did Raghu march dethroning, humiliating and despoiling the kings who opposed him.

Thus having conquered all the Eastern kingdoms, the victorious Raghu reached the shore of the great ocean, darkened with palm trees.

As a cane plant saves itself by following the current of a river so the kings saved themselves by submitting to Raghu who destroyed the aggressive kings.

By his power he vanquished the kings of Bengal possessing fleets and placed monuments of victory in the islands of the river Ganges.

As the Kalam pady yields a harvest after being first rooted out and then transplanted, so the kings of Bengal, who laid themselves down at the lotus-feet of Raghu, being first dethroned and then re-instated honoured him by paying immense riches.

Having crossed the river Kapisa by means of a bridge of elephants he proceeded towards Kalinga the road to which was pointed out by the inhabitants of Utkala.

As a driver strikes the head of a restive elephant with a sharp goad so Raghu made vigorous attack against the mount Mahendra.

As the mountains pelted stones at Indra when he came to lop off their wings so the king of Kalinga, who had a strong elephant force, obstructed Raghu with various weapons.

Raghu, a descendent of the Kakustha family, bore patiently the discharge of Narachas made by his enemies of the Mahendra mount, and assumed the beauty of victory as if on being bathed duly with sanctified water.

His soldiers prepared there a drinking site and in cups of betel leaves drank as if the glory of the enemies in the shape of cocoanut tody.

The king Raghu, who always gained victory by a fair battle, deprived the king of the Mahendra mountain who was first taken a captive and then set at liberty.

Then marching along the Sea-coast adorned with rows of pam trees laden with fruits, Raghu, to whom victory came of itself, entered the Southern country situate under the star Agastya.

The temporal juice of the elephants, and the sweet-scented unguents of his soldiers while bathing in the river Kaveri, lent to her waters sweet perfume and thus created in the mind of her husband the the ocean, doubts about her fidelity.

After doing a little distance the soldiers of the victory-seeking Raghu spent some time at the foot of the Malaya mountain full of Harita birds that frequent forests of pepper.

There the fruits of cardamum plants being ground into dust by the horses' hoofs, flew up and settled in the temples of elephants emitting fragrant temporal juice.

The ropes tied round the necks of elephants, which were tearing off the shackles of their feet, being bound to the grooves made on the trunks of the Sandal trees by the serpents winding round them did not become loosened.

The heat of the sun is diminished when he is in the south, but the Pandya kings of that quarter could not stand before the power of Raghu.

They saluted the feet of Raghu and presenting him with costly pearls found at the conjunction of the river Tamraparni and the great ocean appeared to give them their amassed glory.

Having enjoyed the mount Malaya covered with Sandal trees as well as the mount Durdur, both constituting as it were the breasts of the South, the irrepressible king crossed the mount Sahya which looked like the waist of a damsel shorn of the cloth on account of the receding of the ocean.

When his four-fold army went out to conquer the kings of the West, the great sea, which had been made to retire from the mount Sahya by the arms of Purasurama, appeared once more to touch it.

Disregarding personal decorations the terrified Kerala women fled away before him. And as at times they looked behind, the dust deposited on their locks, looked like powder of red arsenic. Carried by the cool breeze of the river Murala, the dust of the Ketaki flowers, falling on the weapons of Raghu's soldiers, acted as unsolicited perfume.

The sound of the trappings of horses, when on speed, defeated the murmuring noise of *Rajtali* trees shaken by the wind.

Leaving the Punnaga flowers, swarms of black bees sat on the temples of elephants, perfumed with temporal juice, tied to the trunks of the date trees.

At the request of Jamadagni's son the ocean had gone to a great distance, but it now paid its tribute through the western kings.

Being cut and covered with inscriptions by the tusks of the maddened elephants the Trikuta mountain formed as it were a high monument of victory in that quarter.

As a Yogin follows the path of divine knowledge to vanquish his enemies the senses so Raghu proceeded by an inland route to defeat the Persians.

As untimely clouds cannot bear the heat of the new sun which gives red tint to the lotus so he could not bear the crimson colour, caused by the drinking of wine, of the lotus countenances of Yavana women.

A great encounter took place between him and the Yavanas having cavalry. And the field being enshrouded in darkness the two armies marked their respective positions from the twang of their bows.

Being cut off by his spears the bearded heads of of the Yavanas covered the earth like so many bee-hives.

Taking off their head-gears the remaining Yavana soldiers prayed for mercy which was shown to them for anger of the great is appeas ed by submission.

Having spread excellent seats of skin on a site

surrounded with vine his soldiers removed the fatigue of victory with wine.

Raghu then proceeded to the North to vanquish the northern princes by the power of his arms like the sun, who during the northern solistice, draws by his rays the moisture of the earth.

His horses removed their fatigue by rolling on the banks of the Indus flowing through Cashmere and shook their manes reddened with powder of Kumkuma, grown on its banks.

Raghu displayed so great a power in killing the Hunas of the north that their wives reddened their white checks by striking them with their hands.

Unable to bear the power of Raghu the Kambhoja kings prostrated themselves before him like Akshata tree bruised by his elephants tied to them.

He constantly received tributes in the shape of the most excellent horses and heaps of gold ; but they could not come before him.

Then Raghu, escorted by his cavalry, got upon the mount Himalaya. The dust of red earth and other minerals raised by his horses' hoofs seemed to increase the bulk of their summits.

The lions lying in caves, that were equally powerful like the king, did not get up on hearing the shouts of the soldiers but simply looked on fearlessly.

The breeze, causing sound of bamboos, the murmering noise of Bhurja leaves, and carrying the spray of the Ganges, served him on the way.

His troopers enjoyed rest under the shade of Nameru trees on rocks perfumed with the musk of deer that had lain on it before.

Reflecting their effulgence on the neck-chains of the elephants tied to Sarala trees, the herbs, growing on the Himalaya, served the purpose of oil-lamps to Raghu in the night.

At stages left by him, the fir-trees, bruised by the neck-chains of elephants, described to the Kinnars the size of those animals.

There a great encounter took place between Raghu and the Ganas of the mountains in which *naraches*, *vindipalas* and stones caused fire by striking against one another.

Having compelled by arrows the *Utsavsanketas*, to terminate their festivities he made the Kinnaras sing the glories of his victorious arms.

From the presents brought for him by the mountaineers he formed an estimate of Himalaya's wealth and who also formed an idea of the king's power.

Having established his own undecaying fame there the king got down from the Himalaya without attacking, out of contempt, the mount Kailasha which was once shaken by Pulasta's son Ravana and thus making it ashamed.

He then crossed the Lauhitya and the king of Pragyotish began to tremble as well as the black Aguru trees to which the elephants of that victorious king were tied.

What to speak of bearing the attack of the soldiers he could not even withstand the sight of the dust which was raised by Raghu's car-wheels and which resembled an inclement day with the sun enshrouded in clouds but with no rain.

On the arrival of the king Raghu who had excelled even the power of Indra the king of Kamrupa sought refuge with him by presenting him those infuriated eiephants with which he used to attack other kings.

With offerings of jems for flowers the king of Kamrupa worshipped the shadow of his feet as the presiding deity of his golden foot-stool.

Having thus finished the conquest of all the quarters and covered the crowns of the kings, unprotected by umbrellas, with the dust of his car-wheels the victorious Raghu returned to his own kingdom.

Like clouds, riches, acquired by the pious, are given away in charities. With the immense wealth which he had amassed after subduing all the quarters Raghu performed the sacrifice of *Vishwajit* in which one has to give away all his belongings.

After the termination of the sacrifice, Raghu, whose ministers were his friends, having removed from the minds of the subdued kings the sorrow of defeat by honoring them with suitable presents, allowed them to return to their own kindoms and wives.

When all these kings prostrated themselves before Raghu at the time of their departure the dust of the floral chaplets reddened his toes which were attainable by his favour and bore the marks of flags, thunderbolts and umbrellas.

CANTO V.

After the Emporor Raghu had given away all his riches in the *Vishwajita* sacrifice there came Koutsa, the pupil of the ascetic Varatantu, after finishing his education, with the object of securing a present of honor for his preceptor.

The king, of extraordinary character, hospitable and highly illustrious went out and received his Veda-knowing guest with offerings in an earthen vase instead of that of gold which he had not.

The king, well-versed in duties and rules of action, who was the foremost of those who value honor as wealth, honored his guest duly and making him seated near him, addressed him with folded hands, saying:

" O thou of sharp intellect, is thy preceptor, the foremost of ascetics, and the creator of mantras, from whom thou hast acquired thy unlimited knowledge as the animate creatures derive their animation from the sun, well?

I hope his three fold penance in which he has engaged his body, speech and mind, and which has made Indra lose his patience has not suffered any extinction from obstacles.

I hope the fatigue-removing trees which you have reared with a father's care and around which you have made water pits have not suffered from storm or forest fire.

Are little fawns, whom the ascetics from affection do not prevent from eating the long sacrificial grass and whose umbilical cords, dropping off, fall on their laps, quite well ?

Are the sacred streams, in which you daily bathe and whose water you offer to the departed manes and on whose bark you throw the sixth part of the gathered paddy, well ?

I hope cows, buffaloes and other household cattle have not entered the hermitage and eaten up the wild paddy with which the guests are entertained and Rishis themselves are supported.

Having trained you properly has the ascetic granted you permission to return home to enter the second stage where one can be of immense service to the community ?

I am not satisfied only with the arrival of such an honorable man as yourself at my court. I wish to satisfy some behest. Have you come here at your preceptor's command or of your own accord to honor me ?"

From the very vessel of offerings the pupil of Baratantu had inferred that Raghu had nothing in hand. Still I worked up with a feeble hope at the noble words of the king he replied.

"It is all well with us, O king. No evil can overtake the people when you are their king. Can darkness enshroud the earth when the sun is in the sky?

It is an everlasting practice in your family to honor those to whom honor is due. But O great king, you have surpassed your fore-fathers in this respect. But I am sorry I have come at a bad time as a supplicant to you.

Having given away all your riches to worthy persons, you have nothing left but your body like the bare stalks of paddy after corn is taken away by the foreters.

The poverty that you have brought upon yourself by celebrating this sacrifice has led to your glory. The waning of the moon when the gods drink its ambrosia gives him greater glory than his increase.

Having nothing else to do, I shall secure my teacher's fee from some ene else. May it fare well with you. Even a chataka bird does not pray for water of the autumnal cloud shorn of its watery content."

Saying it the disciple of Varatantu was about to go away but the king entreating him not to do so, said, "O learned man! what present do you wish to make to your preceptor and what is its extent?"

The wise Brahmacharin Koutsa described every

thing truly to the king who had duly performed the sacrifice, was shorn of pride and regulated the four castes and the four *Asramas* of the Brahmanas.

"Having finished my education I expressed a desire of making a present to my preceptor ; but at first he considered my unflinching devotion to him as tantamount to a present.

Being angry at my importunity and not thinking that I was poor he said " For the fourteen Sastras I taught you bring me fourteen crores of gold coin."

O King, I have been convinced that you have nothing left but the tittle of the king. It is not proper for me therefore to request you to pay the heavy amount demanded by my preceptor as his fee."

Thus addressed by the Veda-knowing Brahman, the sole king of the earth, who was beautiful like the king of Brahmanas (the moon) and who had never wended evil ways, once more said.

" Let not the new stigma visit me that a Brahman's son, well read in the Vedas, having prayed to Raghu for help in making a present to his preceptor, went back disappointed to another liberal man.

O worshipful sir, please remain in this sacred house of three fires as the fourth for two or three days. I shall in the meantime try to satisfy your demand."

With a delighted heart the Brahmana accepted the unfailing promise of the King saying 'So be it." The king knew that there was no wealth available on earth and he therefore determined to procure it from Kuvera.

By the power of Vasistha's mantras with which his coronation ceremony was performed the king could direct his car, like clouds driven by the wind, to the heavens, mountains, oceans and every where.

Desirous of vanquishing Kuvera like an ordinary feudatory chief Raghu enjoyed rest in the evening of the day previous to his departure in his chariot well equipped and with a controlled mind full of pure feelings.

In the morning, on the eve of his departure his treasury keepers astonishingly informed him of the fall of a shower of gold from sky into the treasury.

Having obtained from Kevera, against whom he was about to march, a heap of shining gold resembling a rock detached from the mount Sameru, the king gave it all to Koutsa.

The desire-less Koutsa reluctant to take more than what was due to his preceptor and the king determined to give him more than what he wanted were both highly admired by the people of Ayodhya.

Then having sent that treasury carried by hundreds of camels and mares the king bent down his head for saluting him. The Muni, touching his body before his departure, said.

"No wonder it is O king, that the earth satisfies the desire of the kings who strictly observe their royal duties. But your power is beyond comprehension since you have milked from heaven your desired object.

You have got all the blessings of life. May you like your father who was blessed with an illutrious son like your self, have a son after you. No other blessing can I pour on you for it will be entirely superfluous."

Having thus blessed the king the Brahmana went to his preceptor. As the creatures receive light from the sun so the king soon got a son by the hermit's blessings.

At the Brahma hour his queen gave birth to a son like Kumara. Seeing that his son was born at the Brahma hour the king named him Aja *i. e* unborn after the god Brahma.

He was strongly built, energetic and spirited and naturally tall in appearance like his sire. He resembled his father like a lamp rusembling another from which it is lighted.

When the education of the prince was completed and he was in the bloom of youth, the goddess of fortune enamoured of him only waited for Raghu's permission, as a modest girl, after choosing a husband after her mind, awaits her father's consent to marry him.

In the meantime Bhoj king of Vidarbha sent a trustworthy emissary to Raghu's court to bring Aja on the occasion of his sister's Swayamvara.

Regarding a matrimonial alliance with the Bhoja king desirable and thinking of the marriageable age of his son Raghu despatched him escorted by troops to the rich city of Vidarbha.

Wherever the prince halted on his way to Vidharbha the villagers presented him with tents, bedding, furniture and other necessary articles and therefore he was not the least inconvenienced on his journey through the forest and his halting stages were like pleasure gardens.

Proceeding in this wise on their journey the prince and his soldiers, with their banners turned grey with dust, halted on the banks of Nermuda, decorated with Karanj trees, gently shaken by the cool breeze surcharged with the watery drops of the river.

At this time a wild elephant came out of the river. His cheeks were washed clean of the temporal juice and before he came out of the water, black-bees hovering over the surface of the water indicated his presence there.

Although the red earth had been washed off his tusks yet the blue lines, extending upwards, clearly indicated that he had been busy with the sport of digging up the foot of the Rikshavan mountain.

Contracting and extending his trunk again and again the elephant broke through the high waves as if breaking the bolts of his stable and reached the shore with a great noise.

Having first thrown up the water with his breast

and along with it many water plants on the river bank the mountain-like elephant reached the shore.

The maddening juice which was for the time being stopped by his immersion in [water, again flowed down the temples of that incomparable elephant when he met the tame elephants of Aja.

Smelling the bitter and unbearable smell of that elephat and resembling the milky juice of the Saptachhada tree the war-elephants fled in wrong ways despite the attempts of the drivers to control them.

The steeds broke their reins and fled away quickly; the chariots, with their axles broken, fell on the ground and the soldiers grew anxious to protect their females. Thus in a monent the whole camp was thrown into utter confusion.

Knowing that wild elephants are unslayable by the kings Aja gently drew his bow and struck the forehead of the impetuous animal with a shaft in order to check its course.

No sooner the elephant was struck by the prince's arrow than he was transformed into a beautiful ærial being encircled with rays of light.

Then having showered on the head of Aja flowers from the Kalpa tree by his power, the etherial being, who was an adept in the art of speech, said, enhancing the lustre of the pearl necklace hanging on his breast by the sheen of his teeth.

" Know me to be the son of Pryadarshana, the king of the Gandharvas. My name is Pryamvada.

By the curse of the ascetic Matanga who was displeased with my arrogance I was transformed into an elephant.

Water is by nature cool but is heated only by fire and the rays of the sun. I fell at his feet. His anger was gone and his native equanimity returned again.

He said :—When your temple wlll be struck by the iron arrow of Aja of the Ikshaku race you will regain your own beautiful form.

I have been freed from the curse by you who are powerful and whom I have so long sought to see. But if I do not do you any good in return of what use is my restoration to my own form ?

Friend, I have a weapon by name *Sanmohan* (fascitation). It is drawn and discharged by different mantras. Take from me this Gandharva weapon which secures victory but does not kill an enemy.

You should not be ashamed of what you have done. It was kind of you to have struck me thus. You should not refuse to take this weapon which I offer you of my own accord."

Aja, who was the foremost of men and a master of arms, replied "be it so." Then washing his hands and mouths with the sacred water of the Narmuda, sprung of the moon, and turning his face to the north he learnt the mantra of the weapon from the Gandharva prince freed from the curse.

Then the Gandharva prince and Aja, who had

been made friends by an unforeseen circumstance, parted with each other, one proceding to the garden of Kuvera and the other to the well governed and charming country Vidarbha.

As the ocean rises to receive the moon, so the Vidarbha king, with his heart full of joy, advanced to receive the prince who had arrived at the boundary of his capital.

Going before him humbly king Bhoja conducted him into the city and presented him with his own servants and articles of use so that the spectators regarded Aja to be the host and the king of Vidarbha to be the guest.

With the termination of boyhood Cupid takes possession of the youth. So the prince representing Raghu occupied Bhoja's palace pointed out by his servants humbly before which, on raised altars, vessels, full of water, were placed.

As a damsel, who does not understand the heart of her husband, delays to meet him in the night so did sleep make delay in lighting on the eyes of Aja who was anxious to see the priceless jewel of a damsel at whose Swayamvara so many princes were assembled.

During sleep his broad shoulders were pressed by his ear-rings and the unguents which were on his body were dislodged. In the morning, panegyrists, fo the same age and sweet speech, thus lauded him.

"O foremost of the intelligent, leave thy bed for

the night is gone. The Providence has divided between you two the responsibility of the world. Thy father, aroused from sleep, has put his shoulders to one part do thou now do also the same thing.

Seeing thee under the influence of sleep Lakshmi, disregarding his attachment to thee, passed the night like an unchaste woman, enjoying the beauty of the moon. But the moon has gone down to the extremity of the west, casting off the resemblance between him and thy countenance.

Let thy eyes, with cool pupils rolling inside and and the lotus with black-bees, simultaneously unfold their loveliness and imitate each other.

As if desirous of securing the natural fragrance of thy breath through borrowed sweetness the morning breeze is pilfering the flowers of the trees and coming in contact with the lotus unfolded by the rising sun.

Beautiful, pearl-like, white dew drops are falling on the coppery leaves of the trees, are shining greatly and imitating the playful smiles on thy lips brightened by the sheen of thy teeth.

Before the rising of the sun, the source of light his driver the Aruna has driven away the darkness. O heroe, when thou wilt take the field thy father will feel no necessity of killing his enemies.

Having shaken off sleep by changing sides thy elephants are drawing their chains. Permeated by the rays of the morning sun their tusks, resembling lotus buds, appear to have ploughed the sides of a mountain of red earth.

O lotus-eyed prince, thy Persian horses, tied in spacious tents, are soiling with the warm vapour of their mouth, the rock-salts placed before them.

The flower garlands presented to thee have withered away. The lamps are shedding a pale light and this thy sweet-singing parrot in the cage is emitting the words uttered by us to arouse thee."

As the celestial elephant, Supratika, aroused by the sweet notes of the geese, leaves the sandy side of the Ganges, so the prince Aja left his bed as he heard the well-composed verses of the panegyrists.

Then in pursuance of the rules of Shastras, Aja, with fine eye-lashes, performed the morning rites. And being properly dressed with the help of clever servants he went to the assembly of kings held for the Swayamvara.

CANTO VI.

At the Swayamvara assemblage the prince Aja saw the kings occupying thrones on a richly made *dias* like so many sky-ranging celestials richly dressed.

On seeing Aja, born in the family of Kakustha, beautiful like Kamadeva as if revived into existence by Siva at the earnest prayer of Rati, the kings despaired of obtaining the hand of Indumati.

As a young lion, topping over the rocks, gets at the highest summit of a mountain, so Aja got upon the most elevated *dias* by a flight of beautiful stairs pointed out by the king of Vidarbha.

He sat on a throne set with jems and covered with drapes of diverse colours and looked like Kartikeya seated on the back of a peacock.

Like a lightning appearing as many and playing on the clouds the goddess of beauty dividing herself into many in the persons of the kings was invested with such effulgence that it was difficult to look at her.

Seated on a precious throne in the midst of richly dressed kings, Raghu's son Aja looked as beautiful as the Parijat tree in the midst of Kalpa trees. Leaving the other kings the eyes of the citizens were now turned on Raghu's son as black-bees, seated on flowers, fly off to the temples of wild elephants scented with temporal juice.

Then the panegyrists began to sing the glories of the solar and lunar kings, the smoke of Aguru rose up to the flags decorating the place and the sound of conchs filled the air making the peacocks dance in glee in the gardens hard by. In the meantime the bride Indumati, looking beautiful in her wedding dress and ornaments carried by men in a palanquin and surrounded by her attendants, appeared in the splendid portico leading to the dias.

The minds of the kings were now drawn to the

bride, the cynosure of the hundred eyes, a maiden specially created by the Creator, their bodies only remaining on the seats.

Their growing attachment for the maiden was like the first emissary of their love and their amorous gestures were like the fresh green leaves of the trees.

One king, holding the stem of a lotus, began to whirl it sportively so that the trembling petals struck against the bees sitting on them and the filaments of the inside, thrown up, formed a circle in the air.

Another gallant king, taking up the garland that had dropped off his neck and was hanging being tied to an end of his bracelet set with diamonds, put it back in its proper place by slightly bending his head.

Another king, casting down slightly his beautiful eyes and contracting his principal toe exhibiting the brightness of its nail, scribbled on the golden foot-stool.

Another king, resting his hand on the throne, and raising up his shoulder, began to converse with a friend. For his thus turning his face the necklace, which beautified his breast, touched the upper part of his loins.

Another young prince tore into pieces the white petals of a Ketaki flower, an ornament befitting an amorous damsel's ear, with his finger nails which would have otherwise been placed on his love's waist.

With his palm resembling a red lotus and marked with the sign of flag another king cast his dice resplendent with the lustre of the jems of his finger-rings.

Thinking that his crown was falling off his head though it remained in its proper place another king held it firmly by his hand. And thereat the interstices between the fingers were shining with the lustre of the diamonds thereon.

Then the female gate-keeper Sunanda, who was eloquent and well familiar with the deeds and lineage of each soverign present at the assemblage, conducted the princess first of all to the king of Magadha and spoke eloquently like a male.

This king protects those who seek refuge with him. He is grave by nature and pleases his subjects. He rules in Magadha and is justly named *Parantapa* the aggressor of the enemies.

Athough there are thousands of other kings still by him the Earth is recognised as having a king. There are hosts of stars and planents in the sky but the night is illumined by the moon only.

This king always celebrates sacrifices which the king of celestials attends by invitation. Therefore on account of the long separation from her lord the goddess Sachi has for a long time ceased to decorate her tresses falling on her pale cheeks with Mandara flowers. If you select this king as your husband you will gratify the eyes of the women of Pushapura looking through windows when you enter that city.

When Sunanda spoke thus the thin-built princess eyed the king of Magadha. Without uttering a word she drew aside her garland of Madhuka flowers intersetrung with Durvas and made a cold bow, thus rejecting his offer.

As the waves raised by the wind carry the swans in the lake Manasa from one lotus to another so Sunanda conducted the princess to another king and said to her :—"This is the king of Anga, who although living on earth enjoys the prosperity of Indra. [When he went to the celestial region) for vanquishing the Asuras the celestial damsels also expressed an eager desire for enjoying his youthful beauty. The Rishis, expert in the art of elephant training, trained his elephants.

Having caused heavy drops of tears to fall on the breasts of the wives of his enemies he, as it were, put a stringless chain around their necks instead of pearl necklaces.

Although naturally living in different places, Lakshmi and Saraswati are living unitedly in him. For his beauty and sweet speech, O fair princess, you are worth of this king and therefore make yourself the third (of qualities).

Hearing those words and taking away her eyes from the king Indumati spoke to her friend's mother Sunanda "let us go." It was not owing to the fact that the king was not beautiful or that the princess could not discriminate virtues and demerits well but that the tastes of persons always vary.

The guard Sunanda pointed out to Indumati another king who, although lovely to look at like the newly risen moon, was umbearable to his enemies.

This long-armed, broad chested and slender-waisted king of Avanti is shining like the sun carefully polished bright on the grinding wheel by Vishwakarman.

The dust, raised by the horses when this king of three-fold power namely courage, energy and policy sets out on expedition, casts into shade the lustre of the jewels on the crowns of the neighbouring princes.

Living near Mahakala where dwells the moon-crested Mahadeva this king enjoys with his consorts moon-lit nights even in the dark fort-night.

O you having thighs like the trunk of a plaintain tree, do you wish to live with this youthful king of Avanti in the gardens fanned by breezes cooled with the waves of the Sipra river?

As the lily does not cherish any love for the sun who unfolds the lotus and dries up the mud by his heat so the extraordinarily beautiful Indumai did not feel attachment for the king of Avanti who was the joy of his friends and the death of his enemies.

Then taking her, whose body was lustrous like the inside of a lotus, who had fine teeth and endless accomplishments, the charming creation of the Creator just in the bloom her youth, before another king Sunada spoke.

In the days of yore there flourished a king, ever engaged in yoga, by name Kartavirya, who used to set forth thousand arms at the time of fight, who had erected sacrificial stakes at the eighteen insular contiments of the world and had been more than worthy of the little king. Whenever any one of his subjects used to think of a misdeed even in his mind that chastiser, with bow in his hand, came before him and put down his mental transgression.

The king of Ceylon who had defeated Indra, lived in his prison sighing heavily, with his hands bound fast with the string of his bow, till the king's pleasure.

This king, whose name is Pratipa, who strictly follows scriptures and the advice of the old and experienced men, is born in his family. He has removed the blame of Fortune that she is fickle caused by the faults of her subjects.

The Fire-god helps him at the time of battle and therefore he considers the sharp edge of Parasu Rama's axe who was like the night of death to the Kshatryas harmless as a lotus petal.

If you wish to feast upon the sight of Reva, through the palace-widow, which flows beautifully even in winter, which looks like the girdle of the walls of the city of Mhaismati, be the consort of this long-armed king.

As a lotus does not like the full moon, freed from clouds in the autumn so Indumati did not like that highly beautiful and charming king.

Sunanda, the guard of the seraglio, thus spoke to the princess about Sushena, the king of Surashena, whose glories were widely known even in the celestial region, and who was like a lamp both to his maternal and paternal famlies endued with pure manners.

This king who celebrates sacrifices duly is born in Neep family. Virtues, naturally hostile, have cast off their mutual conflict in him like beasts when they come to the peaceful abode of a hermit.

The moon-like effulgence of his person which gives pleasure to the eyes, falls in his own house and his heroic power falls on the house of his enemy and covers its top with a net of arrows.

Whitened by the sandal pastes decorating the breasts of the women of his seraglio while sporting in the water, the river of black water, although flowing from Mathura, appears to have received the water of the Ganges.

With the jewel which sheds its lustre on his breast and which was given him by the serpent Kalya living in Jamuna when frightened by Garuda he overclouds even Krishna with his costly Koustava jem.

O fair princess, selecting this prince as your husband spend your days happily in Vrindavana where beds are made of tender leaves, strewn with flowers and which is in no wise inferior to the garden of Kuvera.

Sitting on a rock cooled with water and scented with mountainous herbs in the charming valley of Govardhana hill do you enjoy the pleasure of seeing the peacocks dance in the rainy season.

Indumati, possessing a navel beautiful like an eddy, who was destined to be another's wife, passed by that king, like an ocean-going river with a beautiful eddy changing its course on coming across a hill.

When the maiden princess, having a full-moon-like countenance, came to Hemangada, the king of Kalinga, whose arms were decorated with bracelets and who had rooted out his foes, the maid-servant said.

This king, whose strength is impregnable like the mount Mahendra, is the master of the Mahendra mountain and the great sea. When he goes out on an expedition the mount Mahendra, with its fountains as if precedes him like an elephant exuding juice.

This king, possessed of beautiful arms, the foremost of bowmen, bears on his two arms two black lines caused by the constant rubbing of bow strings, like two torrents of the tears of the damsels of the enemies taken captives mixed with collyrium.

When lying asleep in his palace, the ocean adjacent to it, awakens him, the waves of which can be seen from the palace window and whose deep sound dispensed with the necessity of ringing bells to announce different hours.

The drops of perspiration being removed from your body by the winds which carry away flowers of Lavanga trees from other islands, sport you with this king on the sea-shore which is filled with the sound of the Tati trees.

The youngest sister of the Bhoja Raj, who is attracted by real beauty, went away from the king though she was tempted by the maid, like the goddess of prosperity from a person whose luck s bad, drawn near by manliness.

Then approaching the king of Nagpur, beautiful like a celestial the female door-keeper Sunada said to the daughter of the Bhojaraj :—" O you having eyes like those of Chakora, look at this king.

He is the king of the Pandu kingdom. With pearl chains hanging on his shoulders, and breast pasted with gold coloured sandal he is shining like the king of mountains abounding in springs and stricken with the rays of the new sun.

Agastya, who had obstructed the growing height of the Vindhya mountain, who had, with one pamful, drunk up the great sea and vomitted out it again, affectionately enquires of this king when he stands with body wet after the celebration of the horse sacrifice, if the bathing ceremony had been properly done.

5

Having made a treaty with him lest he might devastate the province of Janasthana the proud king of Lanka set out for defeating Indra. This king obtained from Hara the rare weapon Brahmasira

This king is born in a good family, O fair damsel, if he formally marries you, you will be a co-wife with the southern quarter abounding in gems and girt by the ocean as her waist chain.

O you having good sense, sport happily in the valleys of Malaya Hills where arecanuts are entwined by the betel creepers, the sandal trees are clasped by cardamum and the beds are covered with Tamala leaves.

The body of this king is dark like a blue lotus and your colour is fair like Gorochana. Your union therefore will increase your mutual beauty as that between the cloud and lightning.

The advice of Sunada did not find room in the heart of the sister of the Vidarbha chief as the rays of the moon do not penetrate a lotus folded in the absence of the sun.

Every king, whom Indumati passed by while choosing her husband, assumed a pale look as the houses on a high way are covered with darkness in the absence of lamps.

When she appeared before Raghu's son he doubted whether she would choose him or not but the throbbing of his right hand, adorned with a bracelet, removed his mis-givings.

On appearing before that prince who was perfectly handsome she stopped from going elsewhere. The bees, after getting a blossoming mangoe tree, do not seek another.

Sunanda, who knew full well how to begin or end a conversation, began to say, on finding Indumati, fair like the moon, fixing her attention on him.

There was a king born in the race of Ikshaku, by name Kakutstha, who was Lord Paramount of all kings and from whom the great kings of Northern Kosala inherited the illustrious tittle of Kakusthya.

Riding on the humb of Indra assuming the form of a bull this king appeared like the trident-handed Siva and caused the paintings on the cheeks of Asura women to be removed by his arrows.

When after casting off his bull form the king of gods assumed his most excellent form he sat with him on the same throne touching with his own armlet that of Indra loosened by his driving the elephant Airavata.

In his family was born the king Dilipa who was like a lamp of the house. After celebrating ninety-nine horse sacrifices he did not stop for his inability but for the jealousy of Indra.

During his regeme not even the wind dared shake the mantles of the dancing girls fallen asleep on the road half way from the place of performance, what to speak of others attempting to rob them.

That king's son Raghu is now governing the kingdom. In performing the *Vishwajit* sacrifice he has given away all the riches accumulated by him from the four quarters of the globe and has only an earthen vessel left to him.

It is impossible to gauge the world-wide reputation of Raghu which has travelled over the mountain, gone across the seas, extended to nether region and gone up to the sky.

This prince is born of him like Jayanta of the lord of the celestials. This young prince, although an apprentice, bears with his able father the heavy burden of the earth.

Marry this prince therefore who is your match in lineage, beauty, youth and accomplishments the foremost of which is modesty and let the jem be unite w gold. After Sunanda's speech the princess Indumati looked favourably at him as if receiving him with the wedding garland.

Out of bashfulness the princess could not describe her attachment in words. But it did not remain hidden, but manifested itself by breaking through the person of the damsel of curling tresses in the shape of horripillation.

Indumati thus fixing her attachment on Aja, Sunanda, in a joke, said " Shall I proceed to others." But the bride looked angrily at her.

The damsel, whose thighs were beautiful like the trunk of an elephant, caused the made servant Sunanda, to place the garland, reddened with auspicious powder round the neck of Raghu's son like her love incarnate.

By that garland of auspicious flowers which was hanging down on his broad chest the worthy prince thought as if the sister of Vidarbha has thrown her her arms round his neck.

Pleased at the union of the bride and bridegroom equally qualified the citizens spoke with one voice though it was unpleasant to the ears of the other kings that Indumati was like the light of the moon freed from clouds or the Ganges united with the ocean becoming her.

That assembly, in which the party of the bridegroom were filled with delight and that of the rejected kings were filled with dejection, appeared like a lake in the morning crowded with new blown lotuses on one side and sleeping lilies on the other.

CANTO VII.

Then taking his sister, who, on being united with a worthy bride-groom, looked like the very incarnation of Devasena when united with Kartikeya, the king of Vidarbha went towards his palace.

The kings who were rejected by Indumati became pale like planets in the morning. And speaking ill of their own beauty and dress they returned to their respective camps.

The goddess Sachi appears herself at a Swayamvara assemblage (for destroying those who put in obstacles there). And therefore the kings, though they cherished hostility against Aja, suppressed their anger.

The bride-groom with the bride reached the royal road, which, from begining to end, was strewn with auspicious articles and flowers, decorated with rainbow and where the heat was destroyed by the shade of the flags.

Leaving off the works taken in hand, the ladies of the seraglio, stricken with curiosity to see them, displayed the following gestures on the houses furnished with golden lattices.

Some one, in a hurry to get at the window, forgot to bind her tresses though held by the hand, from which flowers were dropping for the loosening of the knot.

Another, snatching away her feet from the hands of the maid before the dye was dried up, and giving up her slow motion, dyed the entire road leading to the window with red lac.

Another, who had decorated her right eye with collyrium and had not done the left, ran to the window with the brush in her hand.

Another, in a hurry to go, could not tie the loosened waist cloth but held it with her hand and looked through the window, the lustre of the ornaments of fingers brightening up her navel.

The jewelled beads of the half-strung girdle of another woman when she rose up in a hurry and took up and put down her foot steps in difficulty, dropped down; the string only remained attached to the end of her toe.

The loopholes of the windows being covered with curiosity-stricken faces of women having mouths smelling wine and fickle eyes it appeared as if black-bees have sat upon full blown lotuses.

They could not perceive any thing else when they feasted upon him with their eyes, as if the functions of the other senses had been wholly centred in the eye.

It was well that Indumati, after having been sued by other kings not seen by her, preferred the free choice of a husband as conducive to her well-being; or else how could she obtain a husband equal to herself as Lakshi got Narayana.

If this couple of enviable beauty had not been united with each other then the attempt of the Creator in giving them such beauty would have been useless.

Perhaps Rati and her consort have been born as the bride and bride-groom. Otherwise how could the maiden choose such a becoming husband out of many thousand kings? Mind remembers the pristine unions.

Hearing these sweet and agreeable words given vent to by women the prince Aja reached the palace of his brother-in-law adorned with all sorts of auspicious articles.

Thereupon getting down from the back of the she-elephant the prince shook hands with the king of Kamarupa and then entered into the hearts of women and the quadrangle of four walls pointed out to him by the king of Vidarbha.

Seated on a throne set with variegated jems in that quadrangle the prince received, together with the side-long books of the females, a mixture of honey and a pair of silk raiments offered by the Bhoja Raj.

Dressed in a silk raiment he was conducted by the polite female guards into the seraglio like the white-foamed sea taken to its shore by the rays of the newly risen moon.

Offering oblations of clarified butter and other articles to the sacred fire, and making him the witness, the family priest, like unto fire itself, of the Bhojaraja, united the bride and the bride-groom.

Taking the bride's hand into his own the prince shone like a mango tree entwined by a neighbouring Asoka creeper.

The hairs of the fore-arm of the bride-groom stood erect and the fingers of the bride were wetted with perspiration as if the god of love divided attachment in two equal parts in that pair.

Their eyes, which were anxious to see each other and were casting oblique looks but which were turned away as soon as they met, were suffering from a sort of indescribable modesty.

While circumambulating the fire with rising flames the couple shone like the day and night moving round the golden mount Sumera. Instructed by the divine priest that bride, having a capacious waist and eyes like inebriete *Chakoras*, threw parched grain into the fire, with her face bending low in modesty.

Sacred smokes, perfumed with the smell of clarified butter, Sami leaves and parched grain, rose up from the fire, and touching the cheeks of the bride appeared for a short time like two lotuses pending on her ears.

By the inhalation of that smoke as is the practice the cheeks of the bride became reddened, her eyes were full of tears, mixed with collyrium, and the barley stalks on her ears were withered.

Seated on a golden throne the bride and the bridegroom held on their heads wet rice offered duly by the priest, their friends, the king Bhoja and the ladies whose husbands and children were alive.

The king, the glory of the Bhoja race, having thus performed the wedding ceremony of his sister ordered his servents to distribute presents to the kings according to their rank.

The kings, whose anger was concealed under the cover of external expressions of joy and who accordingly looked like calm smiling lakes harbouring crocodiles inside them, took their departure after bidding farewell to Bhoj and returning back his presents as tokens of friendship.

Determined that that they would take away perforce that beautiful and lovely damsel on Aja's return journey home the kings waited there intercepting his way.

Having finished the wedding ceremony of his youngest sister the king, of Krath Kaisika, sent Aja to his own country, with presents proportionate to his means and becoming the excitement of the hour and accompanied him to some distance.

Having passed three nights with Aja who was known all over the three worlds the king of Kundina came back like the moon turning away from the sun after the conjunction.

The kings had already been enraged with Raghu for having been dispossessed by him of their wealth and now they could not bear the acquisition of the beautiful damsel by his son.

They obstructed Aja in the way while he was taking the daughter of Bhojaraj Indumati as Pralhada had stopped the leg of the three footed Dwarf when it was occupying the space offered by Bali.

Having kept one of the trustworthy ministers of his father's with a large force in charge of Indumati prince Aja encounted the army of the kings as Sona, with rising waves, meets the Ganges.

The infantry fought with the infantry, the car-warriors with the car-warriors, the cavalry with the cavalry and the elephant warriors with elephant warriors. So the encounter took place between equally matched combatants.

Unable to hear each other's words on account of the beating of drums the bowmen did not declare the history of their family but announced their names by letters engraven on the arrows.

In the battle-field the dust, raised by the horse's hoofs, thickened by the car-whels and scattered in the firmanent by the flapping of the ears of the elephants, obstructed the sun like a canopy.

The figures of the fishes painted on the flags of some kings, coming in contact with the dust extended by the wind, appeared like living fishes drinking the muddy water of a newly swollen river.

The clouds of dust growing thick the cars could be known by the clatter of their wheels and elephants by the ringing of the bells round their necks and the friend and foe by the announcement of the name of each other's masters.

When the dust, scattered all over the battle-field, obstructed the eye-sight of the people, the stream of blood issuing from the wounds inflected on men, horses and elephants, served the purpose of the sudden rising of the sun.

The cloud of dust, having its connecting link with the ground cut off by the blood and driven about by the wind in the air, appeared like the smokes that had risen from the fire before it was reduced to red-hot charcoals.

Regaining their consciousness from the swoon caused by blows, the car-warriors reprimanded their drivers who had turned away their steèds and furiously attacked the enemies recognizing them by their flags.

The arrows, of the light-handed bowmen, though cut in twain in their way, reached by their own force their aims with that half that was furnished with arrow heads.

In the encounter between the elephants, the heads, of the elephant warriors having been sundered by razor-like sharp discuses, dropped down on earth after some delay on account of their hairs caught by Sena birds with their talons.

The horse man, who struck the first blow, did not strike again his antagonist lying unconscious on the back of his horse but waited untill he revived. The elephants put out, in fear with the water of their trunks, the fire caused by the unsheathed swords struck by warriors, in mail, against their tusks.

Being strewn, as if with fruits, with the heads of the heroes cut off by shafts, filled as if with cups by the scattered helments of the warriors, and flooded as if with wine by the streams of blood the battle-field appeared like the drinking site of Death.

A female fox, snatching off from the birds a portion of hand the flesh of which was all eaten up by them, threw it off, although fond of flesh having her palate wounded by the armlet.

A heroe, whose head was cut off by the sword of his enemy, immediately attained to the dignity of a celestial seated on a celestial ear with a celestial damsel by his left and he saw his headless trunk dance in the battle-field.

Two heroes, on their drivers being slain, acted both as fighters and drivers. Losing their horses they closed with clubs, and when the latter broke they began to fight, hand to hand.

Two heroes who had been fighting with each other and who died simultaneously, quarrelled over the same celestial damsel when gone to heaven.

The two hosts alternately met with defeat and victory like the two waves of the great ocean alternately raised by two opposite winds.

On his army being routed by the enemy the powerful Aja rushed upon his foes as the fire remains where the fuel is, no matter where the smoke is carried by the wind.

As the great boar, at the end of the cycle, threw back the rising waves, so the heroic Aja, having none to help him, riding on his car and equipped with his armour, bow and quiver, withstood the attack of the kings.

The people saw him place his right hand calmly in the mouth of the quiver. Then the bowstring that warrior, drawn once to his ears, poured forth arrows destructive of enemies.

He covered the earth with the heads of the enemies in which the lips were excessively red for being bitten in anger, which bore distinct and ascending marks of the contraction of eye brows, cut off by him with loud roars with *bhallas.*

Concentrating their physical and mental strength, and collecting their fourfold forces the kings simultaneously attacked him with their mail-piercing weapons.

Just as a dawn covered with mist is known by the faintly visible sun, so his car, enshrouded with the arrows of the enemy was visible by the flags at its top.

The energetic son of the Lord Paramount, beautiful like Kandarpa, discharged at the kings the *Sanmohana* weapon received by him from the Gandharva Pryamvada.

The armies of the kings were at once possessed by deep sleep, their bodies resting motionless against flag-staffs, their head gears slipping down and their hands inert in drawing bows.

Then putting the conch to his lip which would be kissed by his wife the prince blew it. While blowing it the heroe of heroes, seemed to be drinking the living fame acquired by his own self.

Aja's soldiers, when they returned to the field, recognised that blaze and saw him among the stupilied enemies shining like the image of the moon in the midst of the folded lotuses.

Aja caused the following words to be written on the flags of the kings with arrow heads dipped in blood :—The son of Raghu has robbed you of your glory but not of your life through mercy.

With one of his arms resting on an end of the bow, with hairs dishevelled by the pulling off of his helmet, and his brows covered with drops of perspiration Aja spoke to his terrified consort.

"O princess of Vidarbha, look at the enemies who can be robbed of their arms even by boys. I order you to do so. They wanted to take you from me by such-like war feats.

Shorn of the gloom cast by the enemy her countenance shone like a mirror which regains its brightness when the dimness caused by breath is gone.

Though highly pleased she congratulated her lover through her maids and not by herself as she felt abashed, just as the earth, soaked by the drops of the new rains, expresses her joy to the clouds by the cries of peacocks.

Having thus trampled the kings under his left foot and been freed from shame Aja took his accomplished wife home. With her hairs covered with dust raised by the horses of the car she looked like his goddess of victory.

Raghu, who had been informed before of all this, congratulated his son who came back victorious with his praiseworthy wife. And transmitting the charge of his people to his care he became anxious to follow the paths of peace and emancipation. When their sons became able to take the burden of the family the kings of the solar dynasty never remained in their homes.

CANTO VIII.

Before the wedding thread was removed from the hand of the beautiful prince Aja the king Raghu handed over to him the earth like the second Indumati herself.

The other princes, by administering poison and taking recourse to other sinful practices, attempt to get by their kingdoms, but Aja took charge of it, only because he was ordered by his father to do so and not for enjoying pleasures.

Being sprinkled with sacred water by the great Rishi Vasistha the earth and the queen, after going through the ceremony of being sprinkled along with Aja, by their joy so clearly seen, expressed their success of having a becoming husband.

According to the rules laid down in the Atharva Veda the family priest Vasistha performed the Abhiseka ceremony of the heir-apparent. He gradually grew irrepressible to his enemies, for when Kshatriya prowess is united with the Brahma energy it becomes like the union of fire and wind.

Having obtained the youthful Aja as their king the subjects thought that they had] got Raghu, with youth returned to him, as their king, for the prince not only inherited the prosperity of his sire but all his accomplishments too.

At that time two auspicious objects, being united with another two auspicious objects, assumed greater beauty. As passing into the hands of Aja his highly prosperous ancestral kingdom appeared beautiful so his youthfulness, united with his humble character, appeared graceful.

The king Aja, endued with incomparable strength of arms, began to enjoy mildly the newly acquired earth like unto a newly married wife lest a least oppression might upset her.

As hundreds of rivers are not insulted by a great ocean so no one met with insult from the king Aja. Therefore all his subjects were, day and night, engaged in works conducive to his well-being and pleasure.

He was neither very hot-tempered nor very excessively mild. In sooth adopting a middle course he gradually brought the kings to his submission without ruining them entirely, as the wind, without either breaking down or uprooting the trees, bends them down only.

Thereupon seeing his son devoid of avarice, self-controlled and encircled by his subjects, the king

Raghu gave up his attachment for the transient objects of the world.

The kings, born in the race of Dilipa, used to hand over the charge of the kingdom, in their old age, to their sons and controlling their minds led the lives of ascetics clad in bark.

But beholding his sire Raghu about to retire into the forest, and saluting his feet with his head adorned with a head-gear the prince Aja prayed to him, saying " Do not repair to the forest leaving me behind."

Thereat moved by the piteous accents and tears of the prince, Raghu, fond of his son, agreed to satisfy his desire. But as a serpent does not take back the cast off slough so he did not take back the prosperous kingdom handed over to his son.

Adopting the final stage of life and controlling his senses he began to live in a solitary site at the outskirt of the city. And the goddess of fortune, enjoyed by his son, began to serve him like a daughter-in-law.

The old king Raghu began to wend the path of beatitude and the new king Aja began to travel by the road of advancement. So like the sky assuming a wonderful appearance when the moon sets and the sun rises the royal family looked highly beautiful.

People regarded Raghu, bearing marks of a king and an ascetic and his son as the two divisions of religion, *viz.*, *Nivritti* (inaction) productive of emancipation and *Pravritti* (action) productive of great advancement, incarnated on earth.

In order to make fresh conquests of territories never conquered before the king Aja became united with ministers, expert in political counsels. King Raghu too, in order to attain emancipation, lived in the company of ascetics conversant with the knowledge of Brahma.

For governing his subjects the youthful king sat on his seat of judgment and the old king Raghu sat on a seat of Kuca grass in a solitary place for practising concentration of mind.

One high-souled king, by the prowess of his wealth and arms, began to subdue the external kings and the other great man (Raghu) by means of devout meditation began to suppress the five vital airs.

The youthful king Aja baffled all the works undertaken by the other kings of the world ; the old king too, by the fire of his divine knowledge, reduced into ashes all his Karma, the cause of repeated births in this world.

Considering the result of his action the youthful king made use of six means, treaty etc ; the old king, looking impartialiy on gold and a clod of earth and controlling his mind continually, conquered the three *gunas*, Sattwa, Rajas and Tamas.

The new king never refrained from vigorously carrying on a work undertaken by him till he obtained the fruits thereof. The old king, of fixed mind, did not abstain from Yoga practices till he saw the *Paramatman*.

Having thus suppressed the selfish actions of the senses and enemies they both engaged their minds in the matters of emancipation and worldly advancement and obtained three-fold Siddhis.

Afterwards Raghu, looking impartially on all, spent a few years at Aja's request and then attained by Yoga to the station of the Eternal Great Purusha standing above the cosmic illusion.

Hearing of the demise of his sire and shedding tears continually Raghu's son, who kept sacred fire, interred his dead body with the ascetics and did no perform the cremation ceremony which was against the practice of the Sanyasins.

Such great souls, [following the path of emancipation, do not long for *Pindas* offered by their sons. Although informed of it, Aja, conversant with the rites of the Sraddha ceremony, performed his obsequial rites out of his respectful love for his father.

After having been consoled by persons, conversant with divine knowledge saying " It is not proper for one to grieve for his father who has attained emancipation" Aja cast off a little his sorrow for his father. And putting arrow to his bow he established his sole sovereignty all over the world and governed it in great happiness.

Having obtained the highly powerful king Aja

as their lord the earth abounded in jems and Indumati gave birth to a heroic son.

This son was Dasharatha. He was effulgent like the sun of thousand rays and his fame travelled all over the ten quarters. The learned recognised him as the father of Rama, the slayer of the ten-headed Ravana.

Being freed severally from the debts to the Rishis, gods and departed manes by means of Vedic studies, sacrifices and a son he shone greatly like the sun freed from the halo around it.

His manliness was devoted to the relief of the distressed and to the proper rewarding of persons well read in scriptural literature. It was not his wealth only that was spent for helping others but all his qualities too were devoted to the same work.

Having looked after the house-hold duties and left the kingdom in charge of his son one day king Aja began to enjoy the company of his queen Indumati in a garden near the city like unto Indra enjoying the company of Sachi in the garden of Nandana.

At that time the great Saint Narada, conversant with three times, was passing by the etherial way for worshipping, with the music of his Vina, the Lord Bholanath, the husband of Bhavani, ever existent, intelligent and blissful, established at the sacred shrine of Gokarna situate on the bank of the southern ocean.

On the top of his Vina was hanging a charming garland of celestial flowers. The powerful wind, as if attracted by its sweet scent, pilfered it.

The black-bees began to follow the flowers of the garland at which it appeared that the *Vina*, of the great Rishi, insulted by the wind, was shedding tears polluted by collyrium.

Having overpowered the beauty of the trees and creepers of that garden, produced by the season, the garland enjoyed ease after dropping on the nipples of the breasts of the beloved queen Indumati.

As soon as she saw that celestial garland which was but the temporary companion of her well-formed breasts the queen became bewildered and shut up her eyes like the moon possesed by Rahu.

Along with the unconscious body of his dearest consort the king also dropped down. It is a well known fact that whenever a drop of oil falls down from the wick of a lamp a part of the burning flame also drops down.

Hearing the piteous cries of the attendants of the royal pair, the geese, Sarasas and other birds, living in that lake, began to cry also out sympathy for them.

Thereupon with water and fanning the fainting fit of the king was a little abated, but the queen remained in that state. Curative measures act successfully only when still lingers there a part of the lease of life.

Then the king Aja, greatly attached to his most

beloved queen, took her up on his own lap ever familiar to her, who was like unto a Vina, before the string is set, for the loss of consciousness.

All the senses being inert the limbs of Indumati had become pale. Therefore by placing her on his lap the king appeared like the morning moon bearing the soiled mark of a hare.

Casting off his natural forbearance in the absence of his dearest consort he began to bewail in accents suppressed by tears.

" What to speak of man composed of flesh and blood, even the hardest iron is heated and melted by fire."

Looking at that garland of flowers the king began to say piteously. " If this tender flower can destroy life as soon as it touches a body then what article of the Destroyer is there which cannot kill a person ?

The destroyer Kritanta destroys a tender article with another tender thing. Herein is the example of a lotus which is killed by the fall of dews.

If this garland of flowers had killed her all on a sudden, why does it not kill me though I have placed it for a long time on my breast ? I understand, by the will of the Providence, some time a poison is changed into ambrosia and again elsewhere ambrosia is changed into poison.

For my ill luck the Creator has created this thunder which, without killing the tree, has destroyed the creeper resting on it."

Thereupon casting his looks upon the dead body of Indumati, the king, ever fond of his wife, said "O dear, you never showed me any disregard although I had comitted a hundred offences but I have committed no offence today. Why dont you welcome me then?

O you of pure smiles, methinks you knew me to be a cheat and dishonest fellow, or else why have you left this world without taking leave of me?

Alas! This cursed life once followed my dearest. Why has it come back again after leaving her? Let it suffer this dreadful pang of separation by its own fault.

O dear, still the drops of perspiration, caused by sexual enjoyment, lie on your lotus face. But where have you gone yourself leaving aside your body? Oh fie on this worthlessness of the body.

O you having a moon-like countenance, formerly I had never in my mind done any thing unpleasant to you. Why have you forsaken me then? In name only I am the lord of the earth, but in sooth my love is firmy fixed on you.

O you having thighs like the trunk of an elephant, the wind shaking your curling tresses black like bees and set with flowers methinks you have revived.

O dearest, as herbs, being lighted up in the night, remove the darkness of the Himalayan caves, so do you, regaining your consciousness in no time, remove my misery. Do not afflict me thus.

The curling locks are being shaken on your countenance but your mouth has desisted from speaking; like unto a lotus of a hundred petals with black bees sleeping in the night it is paining me continually.

Because the night regains the moon and the female Chakravaka its mate and therefore they can withstand the separation. But you have forsaken me for good and this is scorching my body.

Lying down on a tender and delightful bed of new leaves your soft and beautiful body used to suffer pain. How will it suffer today the terrible pang of rising on the funeral pyre ?

With the termination of your happy movements, this your first and dearest companion of the sexual intercourse, your tongue is speechless. Finding you engaged in deep slumber from which you will never awake she looks as if also dead with you.

Anxious to go to the celestial region and thinking me hard enough to bear separation you have transferred your sweet speech to the coels, your slow movements to the geese, your fickle eyes to the deer, and your playful gesture to the creepers shaken by the wind. But your separation has become too much for me to bear and therefore these accomplishments are unable to sooth me.

O goddess, you thought of uniting this Sahakara and Priyangu as a couple. It is not proper for you to go for good without uniting them.

By striking it with your feet you performed the *Dohada* ceremoney of this Asoka tree for flowers. She will now give birth to celestial flowers. Instead of decorating your hairs how shall I offer them as a garland for your obsequial rites?

Remembering the favour of the striking of your feet accompanied with the tinkling of Nupuras which others can hardly get, this Asoka tree is shedding tears for you in the shape of flowers. In fact, even this Asoka tree has been overwhelmed with your seperation.

O you sweet-speeched like a Kinnari, without finishing the girdle of Vakula flowers, sweet-scented with your breath, half of which you had strung in my company for your enjoyment, why are you fast asleep?

Your dear companions partake of your joy and misery. This your son, beautiful and prosperous like unto the moon of the first day and myself are greatly devoted to you. It is really cruel of you that still you forsake us all.

My patience is exhausted and my love is gone. The spring and other seasons are shorn of festivities. I stand in no need of ornaments and my bed is forlorn. O dear, you were my minister in household affairs, my friend in sports and my dear disciple in fine arts. What is there mine what the ruthless Death has not stolen by pilfering you?

O you of inebriete eyes, after having drunk the

wine tasted by my lips how will you, after repairing to the next world, drink handfuls of water spoiled with tears ?

Know that Aja's happiness terminates to-day although he has immense wealth. No other tempting object will attract my mind. My enjoyment of worldly objects is subject to you."

Having thus bewailed piteously for his dear wife Aja, the king of Koshala, made also the trees sullied with tears in the shape of juice trickling down from their branches.

Having removed from the lap of Aja with difficulty, the all-beautiful Indumati adorned with that death ornament of the celestial garland, his kinsmen consigned her to the fire lighted with Aguru and sandal woods.

Fearing the censure that Aja, although a king, yet followed his wife in death out of grief he did not reduce his body to ashes along with that of his dear wife but he had not the least desire to live.

After ten days the learned king Aja performed with great eclat in that garden near the city the Sraddha ceremony of Indumati whose accomplishments only then remained.

Being pale like the moon in the end of the night on account of the separation of his dearest wife he entered the city seeing his own sorrow in the eyes of the damsels thereof.

Although living in his own hermitage being initiated into a sacrifice the great ascetic Vasistha came to know of the stupifying grief of Aja and communicated to him the following consoling words through one of his disciples.

Approaching the king the disciple said :—O king, Lord Vasistha is engaged in a sacrifice which is not yet finished. Therefore although informed of the cause of your sorrow he has not been able to come here in person.

O you of good temper, he has communicated to you the following short advice. O illustrious king, listen to the message of the great Rishi and bear it in mind.

With the unobstructed eyes of knowledge the great Rishi sees the present, past and future of the three worlds.

O king, formerly terrified at the hard ascetcism carried on by the great saint Trinavindu, the king of gods despatched to him a celestial damsel by name Harini for breaking his devout meditation.

Coming before that ascetic Harini displayed various charming and lustful gestures. Inflamed with anger consequent upon his ascetic observances being obstructed, like unto fire of dissolution in the ocean of peace, he imprecated a curse on her, saying "Go and be born as a woman."

Hearing of that curse Harini prostrated herself at the feet of that great Muni and said with folded palms:—O lord, I am another's servant. Dost thou forgive me if I have acted against thee." Being pleased with her humble words the great saint said. "Seeing celestial flowers you will cast off your human body and repair again to the celestial region."

O king, that Harini was born as Indumati in the family of Krathakaishika and became your consort. And beholding the celestial flowers, the agent for releasing her from the curse, dropped from the sky, she has cast off her body.

It is useless to grieve for her. Death is certain when a person is born. Do you now govern this earth, for the kings have the earth for their wife.

Without being addicted to sensual pleasures you acquired true knowledge in your youth by studying the spiritual science. Taking recourse to patience in this your mental affliction do you display again your accumulated knowledge. If you weep continuously you will not have her. If you follow her it is difficult for you to meet her, for according to their respective Karmas, persons, bound for the next world, proceed by different routes.

Removing now the sorrow for your consort from your heart do you propitiate your wife by offering her *pindas*. The learned say that the tears of kinsmen burn the departed soul.

The learned say death is the natural state of the bodied beings—and birth is merely a disordered state. It is so much an acquisition for creatures as long as they live and breathe in this world. The mistaken people regard the death of their dear ones as an arrow stuck to their hearts but the calm-minded regard it as a door of auspiciousness and accordingly as an arrow uprooted from the heart.

While this union and separation of the body and soul is continually taking place why should the learned grieve for the wife, children and other objects of the world?

O you the foremost of those who have controlled their senses, you should not yield to grief like an ordinary mortal. If the wind can shake a tree and a mountain, then what is the difference between the two?"

Having accepted the advice of his preceptor; Vasistha, the highly intelligent Aja dismissed his disciple. But those words of advice, as if obtaining no room in the heart of Aja filled with sorrow, returned to the preceptor Vasistha himself.

Thinking that the prince Dasharatha of tender age was unable to carry on the burden of the kingdom, the sweet-speeched and the truthful king Aja sometimes saw the likeness of his wife in the oil-painting, her resemblance in a particular object and again enjoyed her company temporarily in a dream and thus spent eight years in great distress.

As a fig tree easily passes through a palatial building so that mace of grief forcibly cut through Aja's heart. Thinking that he would in no time follow her dear wife after his death, he regarded that grief, the instrument of death, which it was impossible for the physicians to cure, as highly profitable.

Thereupon having duly installed the prince Dasharata, humble and capable, who had come of age, on the throne, [and being unwilling to spend his days in misery with that diseased body he made up his mind to die in hunger.

Thereupon having cast off his body at the sacred shrine of the junction of the rivers Sarayu and Ganges and being recognised as one of the immortals he began to enjoy in the company of his wife, far more beautiful, in a pleasure house in the garden of Nandana.

CANTO IX.

After the demise of his sire, the great car-warrior king Dasharatha, the protector of his dependants, the foremost of self-restrained persons and self-controlled, having obtained the kingdom of North Koshala began to govern it by good laws.

On being governed according to the rules of Shastras the subjects of his ancestral kingdom became greatly attached to their king powerful like Kartikeya.

Vasava, the slayer of Vala, pouring down rain in proper season and the king Dasharatha, born in the race of Manu, spending his money in proper time the learned designated them both as removing the toil of husbandmen.

What to speak of the discomfiture arising from the enemy during the regeme of the god-like, energetic king Dasharatha ever devoted to peace even diseases did not prevail in his kingdom and the Earth abounded in crops.

As the earth looked beautiful during the regeme of Raghu who had conquered the ten quarters and that of his son Aja, so the king Dasharatha, equally powerful like themselves, immitated Yama by adopting the middle course, Kuvera by distributing riches, Varuna by suppressing the wicked and the sun by the beauty of his person.

Neither hunting, dice, wine adorned with the rays of the moon, nor youthful damsels, nor any other sport could attract Dasharatha ever studious of advancement.

He never used humiliating words before Indra although he was the king, and never spoke an untruth even in jest; and he was of such a quiet temperament, shorn of anger that he never used harsh words even towards his enemies.

The kings suffered humiliation and enjoyed advancement at the hands of that scion of Raghu's race. He treated them like friends who obeyed his commands. And he used to show hostility with a heart hard as the iron towards those kings who acted against him.

With his bow always set with a string king Dasharatha, in one car, conquered the earth girt by the ocean; his army, abounding in quick-coursing steeds and elephants, simply announced his victory.

When getting upon a single beautiful chariot and taking up his bow he conquered the world the ocean, with its deep rumbling, acted as the victorious bugle of the king, rich like Kuvera himself.

As Purandara cut off the wings of the mountains with one hundred Kotis of strokes, so king Dasaratha, having a countenance like a new blown lotus, with a downpour of arrows shot off his sounding bow, destroyed the strength, army and prowess of the enemies.

As the celestials salute their king Indra so hundreds of kings, with the lustre of the jems of their crowns dyed with the lac of fingers, saluted the feet of Dasharatha of unmitigated manliness.

At length, when the children of his enemies, advised by their respective ministers, appeared before the victorious King with folded hands, he, taking compassion on the widowed wives of his enemies, who did not dress their hairs, returned to Ayodhya from the last extremity of the great ocean.

Although he had acquired the sovereignty of twelve empires, still the Lord Paramount Dasharatha, effulgent like the fire and the moon, always remained careful and attentive knowing the goddess of fortune to be fickle at the least loop-hole.

Having forsaken the liberal scion of Raghu's race, king Dasharatha, the protector of the poor, and the ancient Purusha Narayana the chaste goddess Kamala did not serve any other kings.

As the river, born of the mountains, obtains the ocean, so the princesses of Magadha, Koshala and Kekaya obtained the king Dasharatha, the slayer of his enemies, as their husband.

Being united with those three wives king Dasharatha, the destroyer of his enemies and expert in counsels, looked like the king of gods incarnated on earth with the three powers of lordliness, counsel and energy for instructing the subjects.

Having helped the king of gods in battle the great car-warrior king Dasharatha, after removing the fear of celestial damsels by his arrow, made them sing the strength of his arms.

Having collected wealth from the ten quarters by the strength of his arms, King Dasharatha, shorn of the quality of darkness, took off the crown from his head in the horse sacrifice and adorned the sacrificial altars erected on the banks of the rivers Sarayu and Tamasa.

Having assumed the body of Dasharatha, engaged in sacrifice, clad in antelope skin, holding a staff, wearing a silken cloth, observing the vow of silence and carrying a deer horn for itching the eight-formed Lord Mahadeva shone there highly effulgent.

The self controlled king Dasharatha, who had been purified by the sacrificial sprinkling of water, was a fit person to sit in the assemblage of the celestials. He bent his head only before the king of gods.

Preceding the king of gods with a bow in hand the incomparable car-warrior, the king Dasharatha put down the clouds of dust covering the disc of the sun with the blood of the Asuras.

Then the Spring, adorned with new flowers, appeared as if for serving that matchless king Dasharatha who was worshippful and powerful like Yama, Kuvera and Indra in wealth and energy.

When the sun felt a desire for going to the direction protected by Kuvera his charioteer Aruna turned his horses. Afterwards on the wintry frost being removed, he, making the sky clear, left the mount Malaya.

There arose first flowers, then new leaves, then the humming of black bees and then the singing of coels. Thus Spring arrived at the forest adorned with trees and creepers.

As the petitioners used to run after the wealth of the great king Dasharatha, which was increased by his bravery and political strength and was the sole instrument of benifitting good people so the bees and acquatic birds began to run after lotuses unfolded by the spring.

It was not the new grown Asoka flowers only bloosoming in the spring which excited the sexual desire of people, but new buds also, set on the ears of women, which madden the amorous people, did the same.

Drinking the honey of Kuruvaka flowers which were clever enough to yield milk and were like the leafy ornaments, of the presiding goddess of the garden, made by the spring, the bees began to hum.

The Vakula flowers, smelling of wine, all on sudden growing there for drinking the wine of the mouths of beautiful-faced damsels swarms of bees, anxious to drink honey, came there and disturbed the Vakula trees.

With the appearance of the spring the blossoms of the Palasa trees looked like cuts inflicted by the shameless, intoxicated women, with their nails, on the persons of their lovers.

The sun greatly decreased the fall of snow because it caused pain to the lips of women cut with the teeth of their lovers and prevented them from putting on their girdles. But it did not remove it completely.

With her leaves shaken by the waves of the Malaya air, the Sahakara creepers, adorned with buds, as if engaged in the art of dancing, pilfered the minds of men shorn of anger, jealousy and other passions.

The notes of the Kokilas sitting on the blossoming and fragrant trees in the beginning of the spring were audible like the low voice of the coy women.

The creepers of the garden are singing with the sweet humming of black bees and have been adorned with the beautiful teeth of flowers. The new leaves being shaken by the wind it appears as if they are dancing.

United with their respective lovers the women are displaying many beautiful gestures and drinking honey, more fragrant than the Vakula flowers, capable of exciting desire.

With the movements of acquatic birds emitting sweet notes, the tanks, attached to the houses, adorned with full blown lotuses, appeared like women, of smiling faces adorned with girdles.

The night, corrupted by the spring, and growing pale of countenance with the rising of the moon, looked worn out like a woman divorced from the pleasurable company of her lover.

Having spread pure rays capable of removing the exhaustion of sexual intercourse, the moon, after the termination of the winter, excited the five arrows of Cupid.

The women looked highly effulgent like fire inflamed with clarified butter; and they put on their tresses tender Karnikara flowers, constituting as if, the golden ornaments for the presiding goddess of the garden.

Like unto Tilakas adorning the women, the Tilaka trees, engarlanded with bees sitting on beautiful leaves resembling drops of collyrium, increased greatly the beauty of the forest.

Being adorned with bunches of sweet scented flowers the most charming of trees Nava Mallika, began as it were, to steal the minds of the passers by her smiles blooming upon her leaf-like lips.

The soldiers of Cupid, namely, the cloth dyed with Kusuma flowers resembling the newly-risen sun, the barley stalks set on ear-holes and the notes of Kokilas, brought the minds of pleasure-seeking men under the complete control of women.

The *Tilaka Manjaries*, with white filaments remaining, having rows of black-bees seated on them, looked like nets of pearls set on the locks of women.

The bees began to follow the dust of flowers raised by the wind; which was the flag of Madana with bow in his hand, beautified the face of the goddess of spring and resembled the powders of Kumkuma &c.

Although expert in rocking, the women, being anxious to embrace their lovers while experiencing the pleasure of the craddle of the Spring, had their hold of the ropes loosened.

The Kokilas expressing their minds, as if saying" "O Sensitive women, give up your sensitiveness. It is not proper to quarrel for nothing. If your youth when you can enjoy pleasures once goes away it will never return," the sensitive women engaged themselves in sexual pleasures.

Having thus enjoyed the pleasures of vernal festivities in the company of pleasure-seeking women King Dasharatha, resembling the slayer of Madhu, the Spring and Madana, became anxious to go out a-hunting.

By hunting one learns the art of aiming at a moving body and masters the gestures of beasts caused by fear and anger. Besides the body becomes light by endurance and hardships. For this reason obtaining the consent of his ministers the king issued out of the capital.

Dressed in raiments befitting a journey to the forest the king, placing a bow on his capacious shoulders, set out covering the sky with dust raised by the hoops of his horses.

The king had his hairs tied with garlands of wild flowers. He put on a coat of mail green like leaves. The Kundalas on his ears were shaken by the speed of his horses, and he began to range in the sites frequented by the Ruru deer.

Placing their persons on their creepers and transferring their vision to bees the gods of the forest began to behold the beautiful-eyed king who by his laws had pleased the subjects of Koshala.

By his command the hunters, with rods in hand and accompaned by a pack of hounds, entered into the forest. At that time the forest-fire was extinguished, the robbers were suppressed, and the ground, freed from mud, became fit for the running of the horses.

Afterwards the king entered into the forests, abounding in Gavaya and other beasts & various birds and reservoirs of water.

As the month of Bhadra, filled with the mutterings of clouds, holds the rain-bow set with the string of gold-hued lightnings so the joyful king Dasharatha, holding his bow set with string and twanging it worked up the forest-ranging lions with anger.

At that time a herd of deer, musticating Kusa grass, came within his view. Amongst them the young ones, sucking the milk of their mothers, obstructed the movements of the she-deer. And the haughty antelopes went before the herd.

No sooner the king Dasharatha, riding a powerful charger, and taking up an arrow from the quiver, had gone before them than they, straying away from the herd like lotuses shaken by the wind, blackened the forest sites with theirs piteous looks.

When the king Dasharatha, powerful like Indra, aimed with his bow at a deer, his female mate stood by him, Thereat filled with pity the king, on account of his own desire, withdrew the arrow drawn up to ears. Desirous of shooting arrows at others and seeing their beautiful and fear-stricken looks the king, remembering the glances of forward women, loosened his firm grasp placed near his ears.

Then that foremost of kings pursued the track of a herd of boars distinctly marked by their wet foot-steps who had all on on a sudden come out of the muddy tanks and fled away quickly.

Bending his body a little on the back of the horse he began to discharge arrows. The boars also attempted to return the attack but they could not perceive that their hips had been fixed on the trees on which they took shelter.

When the wild buffaloes were about to attack him he pierced each of them on the eye with an arrow. The arrows went so very quickly through their bodies, that without being soiled with blood they first struck the buffalloes and then dropped down.

Having cut down the daggers off the heads of the rhinoceros with sharpened razors, the king Dasharatha, the repressor of the wicked, lightened the burden of their heads, but did not destroy their lives. He could not bear the supremacy of his enemies but was not against their living long.

By virtue of his training and lightness of hand the fearless King Dasharatha, in a moment, filled with arrows the mouths of tigers coming out of caves towards him like the branches of a Sarjaru tree broken down by the wind and converted them into so many quivers.

As if envying the tittle of the lions, the king of beasts, and desiring to kill them lying in the centre of the herd the lord of the earth agitated them with the twang of his fearful bow.

Having killed with arrows the lions, the enemies

of the elephants, King Dasharatha, the scion of the Kakuthstha race, discharged his debt to them who were the principal helps in the battle-field.

Somewhere turning the course of his horse the king drove towards the Chamari deer. And having deprived them of white chowries with the stroke of *Bhallas* like unto the hostile kings he enjoyed peace.

Recollecting all on a sudden the looks of his dearest wives adorned with variegated garlands loosened at the time of sexual intercourse the king did no shoot arrows at the peacocks of beautiful feathers flying before his horse.

Passing through the cover of leaves the wind, of the forest, carrying fragments of snow, removed the drops of perspiration caused by toil, lying on the face of the king.

Having made over the adminstration of his kingdom to his minister the Emperor Dasharatha, forgetful of other works, grew attached to hunting. Hunting too, like a clever woman, attracted his mind.

Separated from his kinsmen the king somewhere spent the night on a bed of flowers and leaves with the light of the herbs.

Having his sleep broken in the morning by the flapping of the elephants' ears resembling the sound of drums and hearing the sweet notes of the birds like unto the auspicious songs of the panegyrists he began to range in that charming forest.

Once on a time the king Dasharatha, pursing a

Kuru deer, entered into a deep forest unperceived by his followers and by the help of his steed who was foaming on account of the great exhaustion, arrived at the bank of the river Tamasa filled with ascetics.

A sound like that of the filling up of a pitcher arose all on a sudden from that river. Mistaking that sound for the roar of an elephant he shot an arrow capable of putting a stop to the sound.

Although the wild animals are unslayable by the kings still it was no wonder that the King Dasharatha transgressed this injunction for even the wise, under the influence of Raja guñas, wend evil ways.

Hearing all on a sudden the cries 'O Father!" the king was greatly depressed. Then searching for the cause thereof in the forest of Vetasa he saw a Rishi boy, holding a pitcher, wounded with an arrow. And on account of dreadful repentance he considered himself struck with an arrow.

Getting down immediately from his horse Dasharatha, born in the illustrious family of Raghu, enquired of this Rishi boy of his family. Almost dying with the pain of the mace stuck to his heart the Rishi boy thus expressed his own history :—" O king, I have been begotten by a Vaishya on a Shudra woman. My parents are blind. They are practising penances in this forest. Take me to them." Without taking out the mace from his heart on account of the bewilderment of his senses the king, at the request of the Rishi boy, took him to his parents and communicated to them the miserable condition of their only son and his own misdeed caused by ignorance.

Hearing of that dreadful news the husband and wife bewailed for a long time and ordered the king to take out the mace from the breast of their son. No sooner the king uprooted the mace than the Rishi boy expired.

Thereupon the aged ascetic, with tears in his hand, imprecated a curse on the king, saying " O King, as I, in the old age, die of starvation on account of the sorrowful death of my son so you will in your old age die for your son."

Having been thus cursed by the ascetic Andhaka the king of Koshala, who had committed the offence, communicated to him, who was worked up with anger like a venomous snake struck by the foot.

" O reverend Sir, your curse has proved a blessing to me. I have not as yet seen the lotus-like countenance of a son. As a fire provided by woods, although scorching a cultivable field, increases its productive power, so your curse has proved a boon to me; command, what this cruel and humble servant, worthy of being killed, shall do." The king Dasharatha, having thus prayed to the ascetic, Andhaka Muni and his wife desired to follow their dead son and prayed to the king.

" Collect fuels and light the funeral phyre." The king, at once, with the help of his followers, carried out the order of the ascetic. And having his mind depressed by the sin consequent upon the destruction of a Rishi he retraced his steps back from the forest towards the city. As the Varava fire always burns in the depth of ocean, so the curse of the Rishi, destructive of his ownself, was always present in his mind.

—:0:—

CANTO VII.

Having thus protected the earth the highly prosperous king Dasharatha, like unto Indra in prowess, spent a little less than Ayuta years. But within this long time he could not see the light of a son, the instrument for paying off the debts to the departed manes, and capable of removing the darkness of sorrow.

As the origin of jems was unknown before the ocean was churned so the king spent a long time thinking that the birth of a son was dependant on some cause.

Requested by that king desirous of having a son, the self-controlled Rishis Rishya-shringa and others undertook the celebration of a *Putresthi* sacrifice on his behalf.

As the travellers, distressed by the heat of the sun, run for a shade under a tree so the celestials, oppressed by the Rakshasa king Ravana, appeared before Narayana.

As soon as they arrived at the bank of the ocean the Yoga-sleep of the Lord Prime Purusha was broken. The attention of the person sought for is the sign of success.

The celestials saw the Lord Narayana seated on the snake Ananta. The lustre of jems set on the pangs of the serpents lighted up his person.

Covering her girdle with a raiment the goddess Lakshmi, whose seat is a lotus, had her fingers spread on her lap and the Lord placed his lotus feet thereon.

Clad in a beautiful yellow raiment bright like the new sun, Narayana, whom the Yogins delighted to see and who had eyes like full blown lotuses, looked like a beautiful autumnal day in the very commencement of the season clad in a raiment of the newly risen sun and lotuses.

He bore on his breast the Koustabha jem, the essence of the ocean and the mirror of the goddess Lakshmi which, by its lustre, brightened the mystic mark of Srivatsa.

His four arms, long like branches of a tree, were adorned with celestial ornaments, and it appeared that a second Parijata tree had grown in the ocean.

The living weapons which used to destroy the neck marks of Daitya women, were singing aloud his victory.

Casting off his natural enmity with the king of serpents the king of birds (Garuda), whose body was wounded by thunder bolt, stood before him with folded hands.

After the termination of his Yoga sleep, the lord of the three worlds favoured, with his clear and sacred looks, Bhrigu and other great saints who were anxious to inquire after his good sleep.

Thereupon having saluted Narayana, the slayer of the Asuras, worshipped of the universe and beyond the comprehension of mind and speech the celestials began to chant his glories.

"O lord, thou hast created this universe in the form of Brahma. Thou dost protect it as Vishnu and destroy it as Rudra. Salutation unto thee who art of the forms of Brahma, Vishnu and Maheshwara.

As one sweet taste appears as many with the difference of celestial water and vessels so thou, although freed from changes, dost appear in various forms by the influence of Sattwa and other *gunas*. O lord, no one can measure thee while thou dost measure the universe. Thou dost not require a prayer but thou hast conquered all. Although thou art not manifest in thy subtle form still thou art the cause of this entire universe.

Thou art omnipresent and therefore thou dost reside always in the hearts of all. But no body can see thee. Thou art devoid of any desire still thou dost always practise penances. Thou art kind and shorn of misery for thou art always delightful. Thou art old enough but shorn of decrepitude for thou art above changes. Forsooth thy power is extraordinary.

Thou art omniscient but no body can know thee. Thou art the creator of the entire universe; but art self born. There is no other cause of thy origin. Thou art the lord of all, but no one is thy lord. Thou art without the second but hast the universal form.

O god of gods, the seven Sama Vedas sing thy glories. Thou dost lie in the seven oceans. The seven fires are thy mouth and thou art the stay of the seven regions.

The knowledge of the fourfold objects of life namely religious profit, worldly profit, desire and emancipation, the four yugas, and the four Varnas have originated from thy four mouths.

Having withdrawn the soul from external objects the Yogins, desirous of attaining emancipation, meditate on thy effulgent form in the lotus of their hearts.

Although devoid of birth and death stlll thou wert boon as fish &c. Although motionless thou art destroying the sound and although immersed in Yoga sleep thou art always awake. These contrary actions being present in thee who can ascertain thy true nature ?

Thou dost enjoy the objects of sense and practise hard penances; thou dost protect the subjects and at the same time art perfectly indifferent. Extraordinary are thy deeds.

As the stream of the Ganges, though it flows in various directions, ultimately falls into the great ocean, so all the means of acquiring manliness, though variously described in Scriptures, fall into thee.

Thou art the only refuge of those persons, dis-associated from the world, who, for acquiring emancipation, fix their minds on and consign their actions into thee.

As it is not possible to measure the earth, water &c representing thy glory how is it possible to measure thy true nature which can be ascertained by the Vedas and inference.

By remembering thee only people acquire purity. It is impossible to describe the endless fruits acquired by the organs of vision, hearing &c.

It is not possible to calculate the jems of the ocean and the rays of the Sun so the recounting of thy glories who art beyond the comprehension of speech and mouth is not finished even if it is continued for eternity.

There is no wished-for object or aim which thou hast not achieved. That creatures, born on earth, engage in various actions is owing to thy favour only.

That we stop after recounting thy glories is owing to our inability and exhaustion not because we have reached the end of thy accomplishments."

Having thus chanted in various ways his glories the celestials propitiated the Lord who was beyond the ken of senses. That eulogy was the real account of the Lord's glory and not panegyric verses.

The Lord enquiring of their well-being the celestials inferred that He was pleased and said:—"O lord, although the time of dissolution has not come still we have been oppressed by the great ocean of the Rakshasas." Hearing those words, resounding the mountain caves situate near the bank and overcoming the sound of the ocean the Lord, who was without beginning, said in a solemn voice. The goddess of speech emanating from the throat of the ancient poet, the Lord and uttered beautifully and correctly, felt herself satisfied.

That sweet speech, emanating from the lotus mouth of the lord of the universe, being united with the beauty of his teeth appeared like the river Ganges, issued from his lotus feet, flowing upward.

The Lord said:—I have already learnt that the king of the night-rangers has stolen your prowess and energy like unto the quality of ignorance (Tamas) overcoming the Sattwa (goodness) and Rajas (darkness) gunas of creatures.

As the mind of the pious is distressed by iniquitious deeds so my three worlds have been disturbed by the oppressions of that king of Rakshasas. I know this too.

While practising ascetic penances the Ten-necked demon had cut off with his sharp sword his nine heads and reserved his tenth head as a profit for my discus.

As a sandal tree suffers a serpent to get on it so I have borne the dreadful oppression of Ravana grown powerful by the boon of the four-mouthed deity (Brahma).

Having propitiated the Creator with hard penances the wicked Rakshasa, cherishing a contempt for the land of mortals which formed his food, prayed for the boon of not being slain even by the gods.

Therefore having descended on earth as the son of the great king Dasharatha I will offer as food the heads of the Rakshasa-chief, to the battle-field.

You will soon have your respective shares of sacrificial offerings offered by the sacrificers. The illusive Rakshasa will not be able to touch them any more.

The pious men, running in the sky, used to hide themselves in fear, behind the clouds, on seeing the flowery car of Ravana. Let them cast off now that terrible fear; you will soon loosen the tresses of the celestial damsels kept in prison. On account of the imprecation of Nala Kuvera their locks have not been polluted by the touch of the wicked Dashanana.

Having thus poured sweet speech like rain on the

crops of celestials greatly withered by Ravana-like draught Krishna-like clouds disappeared.

As the trees follow the wind by their flowers, so Indra and other gods, by their respective portions, followed Narayana engaged in the work of the celestials.

On the other hand, after the termination of *Putresthi* sacrifice undertaken by the king Dasharatha a celestial being, on account of the presence of Narayana there, came out of the fire, holding a massive cup of gold full of *Charu* with his two hands. Thereat all the priests were filled with surprise.

As the king of the celestials accepted the ambrosia produced by the ocean so king Dasharatha accepted the *Charu* offered by the Prime Purusha despatched by Brahma.

That the king possessed extraordinary qualities was evident from the fact that even the Lord Narayana, the Creator of the three worlds, desired to become his son.

As the sun distributes its early rays between the heaven and earth so the king divided that best of *Churas* full of Vishnu's energy between his two queens Kousalya and Kaikeyi.

The Emperor Dasharatha used to regard highly his first queen Kousalya and was greatly attached to queen Kaikeyi. And hence he was confident that they would give a portion of their respective shares of *Charu* to Sumitra.

Understanding this good object of their husband they each gave a half of their own share to Sumitra.

As a she black bee loves both the lines of temporal juice flowing down the temple of an elephant so Sumitra was attached to both of them, co-wives with her.

As the rays of the sun, called nectar, hold watery conception so the three queens conceived the portions of Narayana for the behoof of mankind.

All conceiving simultaneously the three queens grew pale and looked beautiful like ripened crops.

The queens used to see in dreams that celestial persons holding conch, swords, clubs and maces used to protect them. They used sometimes to see that Garuda, the king of birds, spreading the lustre of his golden wings, was quickly passing in the sky carrying the clouds. Again they saw the goddess Lakshmi, bearing on her breast the Koustava jem given by Narayana, serve them with a lotus in her hand. Sometimes they saw the seven Rishis, after having bathed in the sacred water of Mandakini worship them with reciting the name of Para Brahma. Hearing of those auspicious dreams from the queens the Emperor attained to great delight. And thinking that he would father the father of the universe he regarded himself as the most fortunate and greatest of men. As the one beam of the moon assumes various forms on being reflected in the water of various places and countries, so the Lord

Narayana, without second, began to live in the wombs of those queens dividing himself into many parts. As the herbs acquire in the night light destructive of darkness so the principal queen Kousalya gained in due time a son capable of destroying the darkness of sorrow. Beholding unparalleled beauty of the son the father Dasharatha gave him the name of Rama, the abode of the auspiciousness of the three worlds.

The lustre of Rama's person, the scion of the Raghu family, endued with extraordinary beauty, put into shade the lamps of the lying-in chamber.

As the celestial stream of small breadth shines greatly in the autumn when offerings of lotuses of hundred petals are placed on its banks full of sands the thin-bellied Koushalya looked highly beautiful on giving birth to Rama who lay on the bed.

Kaikeyi gave birth to a highly good-natured son by name Bharata. As humility increases the beauty of wealth so he adorned his own mothers.

As understanding and humility originate from good learning so Sumitra gave birth to the twins Lakshmana and Satrughna.

There was no famine or any other calamity in the entire world. Freedom from diseases and other virtues flourished in the country. Thereat it appeared as if heaven had descended on earth following the Purushottama.

The Lord Narayana having incarnated himself in four parts of Rama &c., the pure wind, freed from dust, blew. It appeared that the four quarters finding their husbands oppressed by Rama to have obtained a refuge, began to breathe.

At that time the fire was freed from smokes, and the sun became delightful. Thereat it was so thought, that they, thinking that their affliction would soon come to an end, had cast off their sorrows.

As soon as Rama was born, the tears of the goddess of prosperity of the Rakshasas, in the shape of jems from the crown of Dashanana, dropped on earth.

The first ceremonial music consequent upon the birth of the Emperor Dasharatha's son was conducted by the celestials by playing on the *Dundubhis.*

The down pour of Parijata flowers made from the heaven in the palace was the first of all auspicious rites performed there.

After going through all the purificatory rites the princes grew up daily sucking the breast milk of the nurses and along with it the joy of Dasharatha consequent upon the birth of sons increased.

As the native vigour of the fire is increased by the oblations of clarified butter poured into it so the natural humility of the princes was increased by good instructions.

By those brothers, attached to one another the unsullied Raghu family shone greatly beautiful like the celestial garden beautified by the seasons.

Although brotherly feelings existed equally amongst them, still the mutual attachment varying Lakshmana was always in the company of Rama and Satrughana was in that of Bharata.

As the attachment between the wind and fire and that between the rays of the moon and the ocean is never slackened so the affection between Rama and Lakshmana and that between Bharata and Satrughna was never shaken.

As the day, covered with blue clouds, after the termination of the summer, attracts the mind of men, so those sons of the king, by their humility and prowess, enchanted the minds of their subjects.

Those four sons of the king shone like four-fold objects of life incarnated on earth.

As the great oceans pleased the king, the master of fourteen quarters, by giving him the entire collection of their jems so the princes, by their accomplishments, satisfied their sire.

As Airavata appears beautiful with his four tusks piercing always the swords of the Asuras, as the Polity shines with four means viz conciliation &c, as Narayana shines with four arms so the king Dasharatha appeared beautiful by his four sons born of the portions of Narayana.

CANTO XI.

Then appearing before the king Dasharatha the great Saint Viswamitra, the scion of the Koushika race, prayed for the young Rama for the destruction of the obstructors of sacrifices for it is useless to examine the age of the powerful.

Although it was a difficult task still the Emperor, who was always at the service of the wise, consigned Rama and Lakshmana to the care of the Rishi, for the kings of Raghu's family even never hesitated to grant the prayer of a person seeking for their life.

At the time of the departure of his sons king Dasharatha ordered for the repairs of the streets of the city. Immediately the wind, with the help of flowers and clouds pouring down water, carried out the order.

Ready to carry out their sire's mandate, the bowmen Rama and Lakshmana saluted his feet. The king too showered tears of joy on the princes about to set out on a journey. Having their crowns wetted with their father's tears the bowmen Rama and Lakshmana followed that foremost of ascetics. The citizens began to behold them with fixed eyes and their looks as if created gates in the highway.

That Muni, having asceticism for his wealth, wanted to take Rama and Lakshmana only with him and for that reason the king did not despatch an army with them but his blessings only which were alone capable of protecting them.

Having saluted their mothers Rama and Lakshmana followed that highly energetic ascetic and shone like months of Chaitra and Vaisakha, brightened for the course of the sun.

As the water swells up and destroys the bank of a river during rains so they moving like the waves shone by their child-like fickle movements.

Although they were used to walk in the courtyards set with jems still by the power of two-fold learning, Vata and Ativata given by the great Rishi they did not feel the least pain in wending the high ways; rather they thought that they were by the sides of their mothers.

Hearing of their past history from the mouth of Viswamitra, the friend of their sire and well versed in Puranas they went on so absent-mindedly that they did not experience the least pain for going on foot although they were used to proceed in vehicles.

The tanks with their sweet water, the birds with notes pleasant to ears, the forest with the dust of sweet-scented flowers and the clouds with shade began to serve them.

The forest-ranging ascetics never experienced that delight on seeing lakes adorned with lotuses and trees capable of removing their toil as they did on beholding the highly beautiful Rama and Lakshmana.

Having arrived with a bow in hand, at the

penance forest of Ananga, reduced into ashes by angry Hara, the son of Dasharatha acted as his representative by the beauty of his person, but could not equal him in work.

Rama and Lakshmana had previously heard from the great Rishi, of Taraka's curse; and now arriving at the unapproachable road shorn of living creatures, by her oppressions they touched the ground with the ends of the bows and easily set strings to it.

Hearing the twang of their bows Tadaka, dark like an Amavasya night and wearing ear-rings of human skulls appeared there like a mass of dense clouds adorned with cranes or Kalika.

Shaking all the trees on the road with great force that Rakshasi, clad in a goblin cloth, attacked Rama with a terrific sound like unto that of the wind rising from the cremation ground.

Beholding Taraka coming, holding a girdle of a man's entrails on her waist and raising up one of her hands Rama discharged his hatered for slaying a woman and an arrow simultaneously.

The hole that was made on Taraka's breast by Rama's arrow hard as a stone, became as if the door, never thought of by Yama, for his entering the country of Rakshasas.

While the Rakshasi, with her heart shattered by Rama's arrow, dropped down, the Prosperity of the king of Lanka, well established by his conquest of the three worlds, trembled.

Assailed with the arrow of Rama-like Capid that Rakshasi, having besmeared her limbs with the sweet sandal of blood, immediately repaired to the region of Yama, her lover.

As the sun-jem receives from the sun its fiery power of consuming fuels so Rama received from the great saint Vishwamitra, who was highly pleased, the infallible weapon along with the mantras for destroying the Rakshasas.

Thereupon he arrived at the sacred hermitage of Vamana, of which he had heard before from the great saint. Although the account of his primitive birth, for the want of an instrument, did not arise in his mind still he became absent-minded.

Thereupon having arrived at his own hermitage along with Rama and Lakshmana the great saint Vishwamitra saw all the articles of adoration collected by his disciples. For welcoming that foremost of anchorites the trees of the hermitage folded their leaf-like hands and the deer stood with their faces up for seeing him.

As spreading their rays in order the sun and the moon protect the three worlds from darkness so Rama and Lakshmana, with their arrows, protected that foremost of ascetics who was engaged in sacrifice.

Thereupon beholding the altar sullied all on a sudden with big drops of blood like unto Vandhujiva flowers, at the time of celebrating the sacrific the priests desisted therefrom in fear. The sacrificial ladles, made of the wood of Vikanto trees, dropped off their hands.

Rama, at once taking up an arrow from his quiver, looked up and saw a Rakshasa host, ever obstructing sacrifices, range fearlessly in the sky. Their flags were being shaken by the wind caused by the wings of the vultures.

Thereupon without aiming at other Rakshasas inimical to sacrifices, Rama shot at their leaders Maricha and Suvahu, for Guruda, the slayer of huge serpents, never displays his power at the Dundubha.

Thereupon shooting off his bow an airy weapon, endued with great velocity, he struck down on earth Taraka's son Maricha, strong like a mountain, like unto a ripe leaf.

Another Rakshasa, by name Suvahu, was also ranging there by virtue of his illusory power. Cutting him into pieces with a razor-shaped arrow, Rama, always expert in killing his enemies, divided them amongst the birds in front of the hermitage.

After Rama and Lakshmana having in their way removed the obstacles of the sacrifice the ascetics, praising their heroic prowess, duly completed the sacrifice of Viswamitra, the head of the family, who was observing the vow of silence.

Bathing after the termination of the sacrifice Vishwamitra blessed the two brothers who saluted him with bending low their crowns and touched their body with palms cut with Kuca reeds.

At that time, the king Janaka, the lord of Mithila, invited the great saint Viswamitra to a sacrifice undertaken by him. While going to Mithila the self-controlled Rishi took with him Rama and Lakshmana who were curiously listening to the story of the snapping of the bow.

After wending the way for a long distance, they arrived in the evening at the hermitage of Goutama who was carrying on penances for a long time. There Goutama's wife Ahalya had acted as the wife of the king of celestials for a short time.

By the favour of the dust of the feet of Rama, capable of destroying sins, Goutama's wife, who was living in the form of rock, regained her own beautiful body.

Hearing that Viswamitra had come with Rama and Lakshmana Janaka, the protector of his subjects, came out with Arghya like unto Dharma incarnate with worldly profit and desire.

The inhabitants of Mithila gazed with eager eyes on two brothers descended on earth from the sky like two Punarvasus. At that time they considered even the fall of eye-lashes as deceiving them.

After the termination of the sacrifices marked with Yupas, the great saint Vishwamitra, the scion of the Koushika race, ever careful about opportune moments, said to the king Janaka :—" Rama has become anxious to see your bow."

Beholding the tender body of the boy Rama born in the illustrious and sacred family and thinking of the difficulty of bending the bow and accordingly pained at heart for the vow of his daughter the king Janaka said :—

" O Lord, I cannot allow the young one of an elephant to engage uselessly in that work which even the huge elephants cannot do.

Many a heroic king and bowman, experiencing shame before this bow, and censuring their arms hardened with the strokes of bow-strings, have fled away."

Then the great saint Vishwamitra said to the king Janaka :—" Witness the prowess of this boy Rama the son of Dasharatha. What is the use of useless words, let this bow, hard as a mountain, witness his strength."

Hearing these confident words of the great saint Vishwamitra, the king Janaka believed that it was not impossible that Rama, bearing a tuft of hair on his head, possessed the necessary strength as there is the burning power in a fire of the dimension of an insect.

As the king of celestials orders the clouds to get ready to receive the fiery bow so the king Janaka ordered his numerous attendants to bring the bow.

As soon as he saw that bow the boy son of

Dasharatha, Rama assumed a dreadful appearance like unto a huge serpent. With that bow the bull-emblemed deity shot infallible arrows at the obstructors of the sacrifice who fled away in the guise of deer.

As cupid strings his tender flowery bow so Rama easily stringed that bow hard as the mountain. All the people present there, with fixed eyes, began to witness the great prowess of Rama in stringing that bow.

With a great stretch Rama snapped the Siva's bow. Thereat the bow sent forth such a sound like unto that of a thunder that it appeared that Purashurama, ever inimical to the Kshastryas, was again getting himself ready to destroy them.

Witnessing the prowess of the prince of Raghu family in snapping that bow and speaking highly of his vow thereabout the truthful king Janaka, the lord of Mithila, making the fire witness before the effulgent ascetic Vishwamitra, gave away that maiden daughter born of no woman, the very personification of Lakshmi, unto Rama. Then he communicated a message through his worshipful priest to the king Dasharatha, saying "making my daughter your daughter-in-law do you make the Nimi family your servants."

The lord of the earth Dasharatha was searching for a fitting bride for his son and in the meantime Janaka's priest came before him, for the desire of a pious man is immediately fulfilled like the fruit of a Kalpa tree.

Having duly honored that Brahmana, the self-controlled Emperor, the companion of the king of gods, learnt every thing from him. And covering the solar disc with the dust raised by his soldiers he started for Mithila.

When king Dasharatha arrived at Mithila his soldiers remained around the city afflicting greatly the trees of the gardens situate at the outskirt; but Janaka's city bore that encompassing of love like a damsel bearing the embraces of her lover.

Those two kings, ever bent on showing good conduct like unto Varuna and Indra, unitedly celebrated the wedding ceremony of their son and daughter.

Rama espoused Sita, the daughter of the earth, Lakshmana Urmila, her youngest sister; and then their two younger brothers married the two daughters of Kushadhwaja, Mandavi and Shrutakirti.

Having newly taken wives the four princes shone like the four-fold means of conciliation, gift, dissension and punishment.

Being united in wed-lock with those princes, the princesses considered themselves fortunate. The union of the bride-groom and bride was like that between confidence and nature.

Having thus celebrated the nuptial ceremony of his sons king Dasharatha, fond of his sons, returned to his capital. King Janaka followed them to the distance of three days' journey. Then taking leave of them he returned to his capital.

As the course of a river transgresses its continent and afflicts the shore so one day in the way a terrible wind, scattering the flags and standards, distressed greatly the soldiers.

Thereupon like unto the jem of the hood of a serpent killed by Garuda the terrible sun shone greatly in its effulgence.

The damsels of the quarters put on tresses of twany color in the shape of the wings of hawks, were clad in crimson raiments in the shape of evening clouds and appeared to have been in menses on being covered with dust.

Taking refuge in the quarter presided over by the sun the jackals began to cry hideously as if to urge on Parasurama who offered oblations of the Kshatrya blood to his departed manes.

Beholding that unfavourable wind and other evil omens the dutiful king Dasharatha requested his family priest Vasistha to take propitiatory steps. He removed the fear of the king saying that they will in the end turn out auspicious.

There arose all on a sudden before the soldiers a bundle of effulgence. After rubbing their eyes they, after a while, saw the figure of a man. Holding sacred thread as the mark of his father, and a bow as the mark of his mother he shone like the sun united with the moon and a serpent.

Following the mandate of his sire, who was dishonored and accordingly had his eyes reddened in anger he cut off the head of his trembling mother. And them subduing hatered he conquered the earth. With the bracelet of beads hanging from the right ear he was as if taking an account of his twenty one massacres of the Kshatryas.

Beholding Parashuram, born in the race of Bhrigu, ever engaged in the destruction of the Kshatryas and considering his weak state and the childhood of his sons king Dasharatha was plunged into a sea of sorrow.

That dreadful enemy and his son both bore the name of Rama; and so it was to him like a serpent and a garland of jems—terrific and pleasant at the same time.

Dasharatha eagerly cried for Arghya. But without looking at that side Jamadagnya cast his eyes, having two dreadful pupils like unto the flames of Kshatrya anger, towards where Bharata's elder brother Rama was.

Placing one hand on the bow and putting an arrow into the hole of the fist of another Bhargava, desirous of fighting, said to Rama, standing before him fearlessly.

"The Kshatryas killed my father and are my enemies. I enjoyed peace after having massacred them for twenty one times. But now hearing of your prowess I have been aroused like a sleeping serpent scotched by a rod.

No other king could before bend that bow of king Janaka. But you have snapped it easily. Methinks, the summit of my prowess has been shattered by you.

Formerly people understood me only by the name "Rama" but it has been divided by you; with your advancement I am really ashamed for it.

My weapon can even rive the mountains. Two enemies are equally sinful to me. First Kartavirya stole away the calf of my cow. But you are ready to suppress my glory.

Unless you are defeated I cannot rejoice at my destruction of the Kshatryas. Fire burns even in the ocean as in dry grass. That is its glory.

Know it for certain that you could break Siva's bow because the Lord Narayana lightened it of its heaviness. When the current of a river loosens the root of a tree planted on its bank even the slightest wind can uproot it.

Now put string to this bow and draw an arrow. There is no need of a battle. If you accomplish this feat I will regard you as strong-armed as myself and admit my defeat before you.

Or if you are afraid at the burning blade of my axe then folding your hands, hardened uselessly by the strokes of the string, pray for my protection.

After the dreadful head of the Bhrigu family had said this Rama, smiling, took up his bow and gave a becoming reply.

Being united with the bow of his another birth he looked highly beautiful. The new cloud is itself beautiful and it becomes wonderfully fine when it is united with the rain-bow.

As the highly powerful Rama placed one end of the bow on the ground and stringed it the Kshatrya enemy Parashurama became divested of his lustre like fire with only smoke remaining.

Then the onlookers saw Dasharatha's son of increasing effulgence and Bhrigu's son of waning prowess, confronting each other like the moon and the sun after the termination of the day.

Beholding Parashurama of weakened prowess and knowing his arrow to be infalliable Rama, merciful like Kumara, said :—" Although you have insulted me I cannot strike you mercilessly because you are a Brahmana. Tell me what shall I obstruct with this arrow—your own movement in the sky or the heaven acquired by your sacrifices ?"

Parashurama said :—" It is not that I did not know thy true form, the ancient Purusha. Thou hast incarnated thyself on earth. With a view to behold thy celestial energy I angered thee.

I have destroyed all my father's enemies and have made over the earth with the oceans to the proper person. Thou art the Eternal Purusha. It is indeed a matter of glorification to me that thou hast defeated me. O foremost of heroes, do thou save my course through the sky for going to the sacred shrine. If the road to the heaven is obstructed I will not experience the slightest afflction for I do not long for enjoyments."

Saying "So be it" Rama, directing his face to the east, discharged the arrow. By that arrow a great obstacle was put in his road to heaven. Saying "forgive me" Rama saluted the feet of Bhrigu Rama. Salutation of the enemy defeated by the prowess of his arms is an object of glorification to a heroe.

The virtuous-souled Parashurama said:—"O foremost of heroes, by thy favour, being freed from Rajagunas inherited from my mother, I have acquired the Sattwa-guna of my father's. So thou hast done me good. It is a great favour for me. O scion of the Raghu race, I now depart. Thou hast descended on earth for accomplishing the work of the gods. May good betide thee." Saying this to Rama and Lakshmana Parashurama disappeared.

After Jamadagnya's departure the king Dasharatha embraced his victorious son and began to think out of affection as if Rama had been born again. After the termination of the temporary sorrow king Dasharatha experienced delight like a tree saved from the forest-fire.

Then spending a few more nights in the way in a tent Siva-like Dasharatha entered the auspicious city of Ayodhya along with his four sons born of the portions of Narayana and the four daughters-in-law incarnations of Lakshmi. With the eyes of women of the city anxious to see Maithili it appeared as if hundreds of Kuvalaya flowers had blossomed on the windows.

CANTO XII.

As in the dawn the inside flame of wick, after having devoured the entire oil of the lamp, is on the verge of being extinguished so king Dasharatha reached the end of his life, and was about to attain emancipation after having desisted from the enjoyment of the objects of life.

Decrepitude, as if afraid of Kaikeyi, reached the ear of Dasharatha in the shape of grey hairs and advised him to hand over the kingdom to Rama.

As an artificial stream gladdens all the trees of the garden so the news of Rama's installation whom the subjects loved, gladdened every citizen.

The wicked Kaikeyi had all the articles collected for the installation of Rama polluted with the sorrowful tears of the Emperor.

As the earth, soaked with torrents poured by the clouds, sends up a serpent lying inside a hole, so the wrathful Kaikeyi, consoled by the king, prayed for the two boons promised by him before.

With one boon she prayed for the banishment of

Rama into the forest for fourteen years and with another the kingdom which ultimately brought about her widowhood, for her own son Bharata.

In the beginning Rama weepingly accepted the kingdom offered by his father but he accepted with greatest pleasure the command "Go to the forest."

While Rama put on bark the citizens marked the same unchanged countenance which they saw when he put on silken raiment and they were surprised.

Being anxious to repair to the forest of Dandaka along with Sita and Lakshmana to make good his father's promise Rama as if entered into the mind of every pious man.

Remembering the former incident of the imprecation of the Rishi, king Dasharatha, stricken grief consequent upon his separation from his son, regarded the casting off of his own body as the only penalty for his own sin.

The princes going to the forest and the king breathing his last the kingdom of Koshala became an object of temptation to the enemies who were on the look out for a loof-hole.

Thereupon controlling their tears for hiding the calamity the courtiers, whose master was dead, sent the principal minister and brought Bharata from the house of his maternal grand-father.

Returning to his own house and hearing of the miserable end of his father, Kaikeyi's son Bharata, filled with mighty grief, was not only annoyed with his own mother but also desisted from occupying the throne.

Beholding the trees of the hermitage of Rama and Lakshmana pointed out by the ascetics and shedding tears he accompanied, by the soldiers, followed them.

Communicating the demise of his father to his eldest brother Rama who was living in the forest around the mount Chitrakuta, Bharata requested him strongly to accept the kingdom which he had not enjoyed himself.

When he could not dissuade Rama from carrying out the command of his father then in heaven Bharata prayed for his pair of sandal to make it the presiding god of the kingdom. Giving him the sandal and embracing him affectionately Rama sent away Bharata. Without returning to Ayodhya he went to Nandigrama and began to govern the kingdom, as ordered by his eldest brother, like unto a property entrusted by another.

In this way Bharata, devoted to his eldest brother and shorn of avarice for the kingdom, began to expatiate the sin committed by his mother.

Rama too, in the company of his younger brother of controlled self, and Sita, began to spend his days feeding on wild forests] and roots; in youth he followed the foot-steps of old Ikshwakus.

One day making the shade of a tree still by his

own power Rama fell asleep by placing his head on Sita's lap.

At that time Indra's son, a crow, as if marking the defect of the wound inflicted by the nails of her lover, cut off the breasts of Vaidehi with its talons.

Awakened by Sita's cries Rama discharged an arrow at that crow. The crow, stricken with fear, gave one of its eyes and saved its life.

Thinking that Bharata might again come in the neighbouring village Rama left the mount Chitrakuta abounding in anxious deer. As the sun, in the rains, proceeds towards the south crossing all the points of the compass, so Rama too, resting in the hermitage of the hospitable ascetics, proceeded towards the south.

Sita following Rama, it appeared as if the presiding goddess of the kingdom, disregarding the request of Kaikeyi, and won over by his accomplishments, was following him. Sita so perfumed the forest with the scented unguents given her by Atri's wife Anasua that bees, leaving the flowers and humming sat on her person.

As Rahu obstructs the course of the moon so the Rakshasa Viradha, smoke-coloured like the evening cloud, stood obstructing the way of Rama.

As Avagraha pilfers the rain in the months of Shravana and Bhadra so he stole away Janaka's daughter who was between Rama and Lakshmana.

Having slain Viradha and thought that a bad

smell would pollute the atmosphere if they would leave her there Rama and Lakshmana interred the dead body under the earth.

As the mount Vindhya stood in the same way by the command of Agastha so Rama by his instructions lived in the Panchavati forest.

As a she-serpent, assailed by the rays of the sun, approaches a sandal tree, so Ravana's youngest sister Shurpanakha, assailed by Cupid, approached Rama in the Panchavati forest.

Giving an account of her lineage that Rakshasi requested Rama to marry her in the very presence of Sita, for the growing lust of women does not wait for a proper moment.

Rama, having shoulders plump like the hump of a bull, said to the lustful Shurpanakha :—" O girl, I have my wife with me. Seek my younger brother for your husband."

Lakshmana said :—" Because you first solicited my eldest brother to marry you and therefore I cannot accept your hand." Then she, like a river going to both the banks, appeared again before Rama. Seeing all these incidents Sita smiled. Beholding Sita laugh at her that Rakshasi grew momentarily pale with anger as the still ocean rises with the moon.

" Thou shalt even reap the fruit of this insult. Remember as a she-deer insults a tigress so thou hast laughed at me."

Saying this Shurpanakha assumed a terrific Rakhasi form befitting her own name. Thereat Maithili hid herself out of fear on the lap of her consort.

Lakshmana at first heard her voice sweet like the notes of a coel; but now hearing her terrific voice like that of a she-jackal she took her for an illusive woman.

Thereupon entering into his hut quickly and taking up his drawn sword he cut off her nose and made her greatly disfigured.

With her fingers containing uncouth knots, resembling goads and having crooked nails she, from the sky, roared at Rama and Lakshmana. And immediately going to Janasthana she communicated to Khara, Dushana and other Rakshasas the new discomfiture she had met with at the hands of Rama.

It was really inauspicuous for those Rakshasas to have taken Shurpanakha before them when they marched to fight with Rama.

Beholding the Rakshasas, inflamed with ire, approach with uplifted weapons, Rama, placing his hope of success on his bow and committing Sita to the care of Lakshmana, engaged in battle. Rama was alone on one side and on the other there were thousands of Rakshasas. But in the battle-field the night-rangers saw numbers of Rama equalling them. Rama, the well-behaved scion of the Raghu race, did not forgive Dushana despatched there by the wicked night-rangers. Rama killed Khara and Trishira with the strokes of his arrows. The shafts, discharged by him in regular order, appeared to have been shot simultaneously off the bow. Living in its pure state as before the infallible arrow of Rama, capable of cutting through the body, drank off the life of the three Rakshasas. Drinking their blood the birds justified the existence of their body. There was none amongst those Rakshasas who could rise up except headless trunks. Fighting with Rama who alone shot arrows that great army of the Rakshasas slept for ever under the shadow of the vultures. Then becoming helpless and overwhelmed with dangers Shurpanakha communicated to the king of Lanka, how the Rakshasas had been killed by Rama's arrows.

Hearing of the insult of his own sister and the destruction of the Rakshasas Kuvera's younger brother, Ravana, regarded his heads trampled by Rama. Blinded with anger and deceiving Rama and Lakshmana through Maricha's illusions the ten-headed king of Rakshasas carried away Sita stealthily. Trying his level best Jatayu, the king of birds, could obstruct his course only for a moment. Then searching for Sita Rama and Lakshmana saw the king of vultures with his wings cut off. Communicating to Rama and Lakshmana the news that Ravana had stolen away Sita he died before Narayana himself as if by the force of his piety acquired by his great act of fighting. After the decease of Jatayu the sorrow of Rama and Lakshmana for the death of their sire was kindled anew. Then they performed the obsequial rites of Jatayu.

Rama then killed a Rakshasa by name Kavandha, who being freed from the curse advised him to make friends wfth Sugriva, the king of Vanaras. He then contracted friendship with Sugriva who was like him was also plunged into misfortune. Having killed the highly powerful king Vali by a trick Rama installed Sugriva on his throne which he so long wished for.

Despatched by their king Sugriva the monkeys began to search, like the desire of Rama stricken with sorrow for his wife, for Maithili on all sides.

As a pure man, freed from sins, easily crosses the ocean of the world so Hanuman, the foremost of monkeys, hearing of Sita's whereabouts from Sampati, crossed the ocean and reached Lanka. Searching for her there he gave her Rama's ring, who was surrounded by Rakshasis like a herb girt by a poisonous creeper. When that ring touched Sita's palm she welcomed it with tears of joy. Having consoled Janaka's daughter Sita at the behest of Rama, the foremost of monkeys killed Aksha; and afterwards suffering the oppression of the enemies for some time he consumed the city of Lanka. Having accomplished his work Pavana's son handed over to Rama the jem of insignia given by Vaidehi like unto her very heart. Placing the jem on his breast sent by Janaka's daughter Rama experienced the joy of embrace from his beloved wife for sometime though he could not press her breasts. Hearing of the good news of Janaki and being anxious to be united with her he considered the ocean encircling the city of Lanka as trifling as a ditch. He then advanced with the monkey army for killing his enemy. The soldiers proceeded not only on earth but even in the sky and by other impassable routes. Rama encamped his army on the bank of the ocean. In the meantime oppressed by his brother, Ravana's younger brother, the pious Bibhishana, appeared before Rama. As if out of affection the presiding goddess of the Rakshasas gave him this good sense and sent to him Rama.

Rama promised Bibhishana to give him the kingdom of Rakshasas occupied by Ravana; for policy, when applied in proper time, surely yields fruit.

Rama made the monkeys construct a huge bridge on the watery expanse of the ocean. Thereat it appeared that the serpent Sesha had arisen from the nether region to supply Narayana with his couch. By that wonderful bridge Rama arrived at the city of Lanka and surrounded it by twany coloured monkeys. It appeared that another golden wall had been built around Lanka. Then went on a terrible encounter in the city of Lanka between the Vanara and Rakshasa armies. And victories of Rama and Ravana were announced on all sides. In a fight with trees sticks mounted with iron were shattered into pieces. The clubs were powdered by stone. And the strokes of nails became more dreadful than those of weapons. What more even the elephants were torn by the strokes of rocks. Thereupon one day seeing the cut off head of Rama, the daughter of Janaka dropped down unconscious on earth. Saying that it was the outcome of illusion the Rakshasi Trijata revived her. Learning for certain that her dearest husband was alive Janaki cast off her grief. But she felt great shame that she was alive before when she believed Rama to have been dead.

Ravana's son Meghanada bound Rama and Lakshmana with serpentine nooses. Garuda however cut them off-so the pain was only temporary like that in a dream. Ravana then struck Lakshmana's breast with the mace of Sakti. Thereat although Rama was not himself hurt still his heart was broken asunder by grief. Taking the great medicine brought by Hanuman Lakshmana regained his consciousness and his pain was removed. And again having slain the Rakshasas in battle he taught their women to bewail. As the autumn puts a stop to the muttering of clouds and the display of beauty by the rain-bow so Lakshmana left no remnant of the leonine roars of Meghanada and of his bow effulgent like that of Indra.

Being wounded with Sugriva's weapon Kumbhakarna, resembling a mountain, and attaining the condition of his sister Shurpanakha, obstructed Rama. Saying as if "you are fond of sleep, Ravana has aroused you untimely," Rama's arrow put him into eternal sleep. As the dust of the field was suppressed by the stream of Rakshasa's blood so the night-rangers of Lanka falling in the midst of the Vanaras met with death. Then promising "the earth will either be divested of Rama or of Ravana" the ten-headed Rakshasa came out of his palace to the battle-field.

Seeing Rama on foot and Ravana on his car, Purandara, stationed in the sky, sent a chariot drawn by ash-coloured horses to Rama, the flags thereon were being unfurled by the wind saturated with the water of Mandakini. Indra's charioteer Matali drove the horses. Holding his hand Rama ascended that *Jaitra* car. Matali put on Rama's person the armour by Indra. The arrows shot by the Asuras became bafled at that coat of mail. As if finding an opportunity to display their respective prowess the fight between Rama and Ravana meeting after a long time was crowned with success. All other Rakshasas had been killed and the king of Lanka was alone, still, on account of his many heads, hands and feet he appeared to have been encircled by innumeraable Rakshasas.

Having worshipped Brahma for a long time and afterwards offered his own head as a sacrifice to him the king of Lanka propitiated him and obtained the boon that he would not be killed by the gods. By virtue of this boon he defeated Indra and other guardian deities; and on account of the profusion of his strength he performed the most difficult feat of uprooting the most elevated mount Kailasha. For these reasons the Raghu heroe Rama regarded him as an illustrious enemy. In great anger Dashanana shot an arrow at the right arm of Rama which was shaking indicating his union with Janaki. Riving the heart of Ravana the arrow, discharged by Rama, entered into the earth as if to communicate this glad tidings to the Nagas. They returned words by words and weapons by weapons. And their attempt, like that of two combatants endeavouring to gain victory, increased. As an intervening altar comes equally under the possession of two infuriated elephants while fighting, so success and defeat alternately falling upon them both, the beauty of victory remained equally on the both. The flowers, that were showered by the gods and Asuras on their being pleased with the discharge of weapons or with the act of counteracting them, were obstructed by the incessant arrows discharged by them both. Ravana discharged at Rama the Shataghni covered with golden pikes resembling the club of Yama, which he had acquired by victory. Before it came near their car accompanied with the hope of victory of the Rakshasas, Rama and Lakshmana easily cut it off like unto a plantain tree with crescent-shaped arrows. For striking his enemy, Rama, the incomparable bow-man, set to his bow the infallible Brahma weapon, the medicine for uprooting the mace of grief from his wife's heart. Burning in the sky in a hundred flames that effulgent weapon was seen like the Sesha serpent endued with dreadful fangs. With the strokes of that weapon inspired with mantras Rama cut off the heads of the king of Lanka in a trice. He did not feel the least pain whilst his heads were being cut off. Seeing even Ravana's heads falling in pieces on earth the gods could not shake off their feelings of distrust lest they might be joined together again.

Then showers of sweet-scented flowers, poured by the gods, dropped on the head of Rama, the victor of Ravana and announced his installation. Leaving the temples of the elephants and having their wings laden with temporal juice the bees followed him. Having thus performed the work of gods, Rama, the scion of the Raghu race, loosened the string of his bow. Taking leave of him Indra's charioteer Matali too drove up his car, drawn by a thousand horses and whose flags were covered with arrows bearing the name of Ravana.

Taking Janaki purified by fire and conferring the kingdom on his dear friend Bibhishana, Rama, along with Sugriva, Lakshmana and Bibhishana, started for his ancestral capital Ayodhya on the ærial car gained by him by the strength of his own arms.

CANTO XIII.

On beholding the ocean while proceeding in the flowery car by the etherial way Rama, the scion of the Raghu race, a portion incarnate of Narayana, endued with all attributes, said in stweet words to his most beloved wife Janaki:—"O Maithili, look at the beauty of the delightful autumnal sky adorned with the milk-way and beautiful stars. This ocean, full of foams, has been divided, like the mount Malaya, by the bridge constructed by me. When the great Rishi, stealing the sacrificial horse of the king Sagara, entered into the nether region, our ancestors, searching for the same, dug the earth and increased the dimension of the ocean. The rays of the sun bear watery conception from it and jems are reared in it. This ocean carries the forest-fire and from it sprang the delightful ambrosia. It is difficult to ascertain the form and limit of this great ocean extending over ten quarters and containing various forms like the various incarnations of Narayana. At the time of universal dissolution the Prime Purusha Narayana enters upon Yoga sleep; and destroying all the worlds he is lauded by Brahma seated on a lotus sprung from his navel. As kings, in fear of their enemies, are freed from the same on seeking refuge with a pious king so hundreds of mountains with their wings cut off by the king of celestials have found shelter in this great ocean, the protector of those who seek refuge with it. When assuming the Prime Boar-form the Lord Narayana upraised the earth from the nether region, its rising pure water acted for some time as the beautiful veil of the earth. This lord of rivers, the only enjoyer of streams and an expert in the distribution of the nectar of mouth, by his natural impudence is drinking the nectar of the mouths of the rivers and making them do the same. Widening their mouths at the mouths of the rivers the Timi fishes are throwing up water with the holes on their heads. Look O dear, the water elephants have all on a sudden swam over the surface of the water. The foaming waves, divided into two parts, are covering their temples for the time being and acting as chowries. The serpents are running towards the bank for drinking the air there. They are appearing like huge waves. The jems on their heads being lighted up by the rays of the sun they are being known as serpents. The pairs of conchs, going in an opposite direction by the Vidrum creepers growing thereon, are with great difficulty coming out of the waves.

The clouds whirling all on a sudden while drinking water it appears as if the ocean is being churned again by the mount Mandara. The blue banks of the ocean being adorned with Tamala and date trees seen indistinctly from a distance they are looking till lines on the salt waves of the ocean. O you having expansive eyes, the wind of the bank is decerating your face with the dust of the Ketaki flowers. Perhaps finding me unable to bear the delay of decorating your person, whose thirst is fixed on your bimba-like lips, the wind is quickly adorning you. O dear, by this etherial car we have in no time reached the bank of the ocean. This sandy bank is interspersed with pearls and the trees are laden with fruits. O you having thighs like the the trunk of an elephant, O you having eyes like those of a deer, look back and see the more we are distanced from the ocean, the more it is appearing that the earth with the forests is moving along with us. O dear, as desired by me this car is proceeding sometimes by the celestial way, sometimes by the cloudy way and again by that of the birds. See the etherial wind, cooled by coming in contact with the water of Mandakini scented by the temporal juice of Airavata, is removing the drops of perspiration caused on your face by the mid-day sun. O dear, as you out of curiosity stretched out your hand from the window the cloud, bearing a bracelet of lightning, put on it a second ornament. O dear, look at this Janasthana once infested with the Rakshasas. Regarding it as shorn of obstacles the pious-souled ascetics, clad in Koupin, have built new huts in their respective hermitages once abandoned by them and are living happily. O dear, there is the part of the forest where searching you I picked up a piece of Nupura. Separated from your lotus feet it was silent out of grief.

O you timid girl, the trees and creepers, naturally void of the power of speech, pointed out of mercy by their bending branches and leaves the road by which the wicked night-ranger had carried you away. Renouncing their desire for the sacrificial grass, taking up their heads and turning their eyes to the south the she-deer pointed out that road to me who was not acquainted with the etherial way. Look at the summit of the mount Malyavan touching the sky. Here I shed tears in your separation as the new clouds pour down torrents of rain. Here the scent of lakes filled with the water of rain, half blown Kadamva flowers and the sweet notes of peacocks became unbearable to me stricken with your separation. Remembering your former trembling embraces I could with difficulty bear the muttering of clouds. United with the vapour of the earth caused by new torrents of water Kandali flowers, grown on its summit, pained me greatly imitating the bright lustre of your eyes reddened with smoke at the time of wedding. My vision, going down from a distance, is as if out of exhaustion drinking the water of Pampa lake, covered on all sides with Vetasa plants, and filled with fickle Sarasas. O dear, when I was away from you, the pair of Chakravakas, united in this lake, used to give each other filaments of lotuses. Looking at them with eager eyes I used to experience great pain. Seeing the blossoms of the thin Asoka trees on its bank bent down like breasts and thinking

I had got you I was about to embrace it. But Lakshmana prevented me and my breast was filled with tears. Hearing the sound of golden bells hanging inside this car the Sarasas, living on the bank of the Godaveri, are flying in the sky as if to welcome you. O dear, seeing this forest of Panchavati after a long time my mind has been filled with joy. Alas, here, tender as you are, you nourished the new grown Sahakaras by watering them. Look, the antelopes, reared by you, are looking up at the car. O dear, I remember, in the Vetasa groves on the bank of this Godaveri, with my exhaustion, caused by hunting, removed by the watery air, I used to sleep by placing my head on your lap. Look at the hermitage of the great saint Agastya, who is capable of purifying impure water and who by the mere contraction of his eye-brows, prevented the king Nahusha from attaining to the dignity of Indra. Smelling the scent of Havi proceeding in the sky as well as the smoke of the three fires of the illustrious Agastya my soul, freed from Raja Gunas, has become light. The pleasure tank, by name *Panchapsar*, belonging to the great saint Shatakarni, surrounded on all sides with forest, is looking like the slightly perceptible ray of the moon coverd with clouds. Beholding him live on mere Kusa grass and range with the deer, the king of celestials, terrified at his asceticism, resorted to the vile noose of the youth of five Apsaras. Seated at ease inside a palace built on the extremity of the water the great saint Shatakarni is singing in accompaniment with the music of Mridanga. It has resounded the top of the flowery car. Look, O dear, another ascetic, as if holding the sun on his fore-head, in carrying on penances in the midst of four fires. His name is Sutighna. But he is not fierce but of a quiet temperament. Terrified at his asceticism the king of gods despatched an Apsara to break his Yoga. But her smiling glances, beautiful teeth and other lustful gestures could not disturb his mind. Look, another foremost of ascetics is stretching out his right-hand, which cuts Kuca grass, itches the deer and is expressive of favour, to me inorder to welcome me. He is observing the vow of silence and therefore returning my salutation by a slight nod; he is again fixing his pure looks on the solar disc. There is the charming and sacred hermitage of the ascetic Sharabhanga who keeps up sacred fire. Propitiating the fire for a long time with *Samit* he consigned his own body sanctified by mantras to it. Now removing the toil of the travellers by their shade, the trees, of his hermitage, yielding profuse fruits, are serving him like his sons. See, the mount Chitrakuta is looking like a proud bull. The caves are being resounded by the water falls of the springs. Its summits, covered with clouds, are looking like the elephants besmeared with mud. The river Mandakini of pure water, flowing mildly in the valley of the mountain, and looking small from distance, is appearing like a necklace of pearls placed round the neck of the earth. O dear, look at the beautiful Tamala trees grown near the mountain. With their sweet scented leaves I used to make decorations for your ears white like barley stalks. This is the powerful penance forest of the sage Atri. Freed from the fear of oppression the animals have grown humble. And without blossom the trees are laden with fruits. It is said that for the ablution of the ascetics, Anasua, the wife of Atri, brought down the Ganges here, whose golden lotuses are plucked by the seven Rishis with their own hands and who is like the garland of Mahadeva's head. Standing immoveable for the absence of the wind, the trees, grown around the altar of the ascetics engaged in meditation in Vira posture, are as if also engaged in devout contemplation. This the green fig-tree to whom you prayed formerly; see, the fruits of this foremost of trees are shining like the jems of serpents. Look how beautiful the Ganges, being united with Yamuna, is looking. Somewhere the Indraneela flowers look like a garland of pearls. Some where white lotuses are shining. Somewhere blue swans, fond of Manasa lake, are swimming. Somewhere the water is looking like leaves painted with Aguru and sandal; somewhere it looks like moon-light in darkness; somewhere it looks like a white autumnal cloud. And somewhere it looks like the body of Mahesha besmeared with ashes and adorned with black serpents. By bathing at this confluence of the Ganges and Yamuna, men, even without the knowledge of the true nature of god, attain to emancipation. Look at the city of Guha the king of Nishadas. There when we, after casting off our crowns, put on bark and matted locks Sumantra cried saying "O Kaikeyi, your object has been accomplished." Here is my mother-like river Sarayu. The dust of her golden lotuses adorns the breast of Yaksha women. As Prakriti or nature is the source of the principle of Mahat (greatness) so the Brahma saints consider her to be the source of Brahma. Sarayu, on the banks of which sacrificial stakes have been erected, flows near Ayodha. She holds profuse water purified by the kings of the Ikshwaku family when they bathe thereafter the termination of the horse-sacrifice. My mind is welcoming her like the nurse of the kings of North Koshala who grew up by drinking her water and lived happily on her banks. Alas, separated by the worshipful Emperor, she, as if by the arms of her waves raised by the cool breezes, is embracing me like a son away from home. Look again at this side, dense dust has been raised, smoke-coloured like evening. Perhaps hearing from Hanumana of our arrival, Bharata, with his soldiers, is coming out to receive us. As Lakshmana returned you to me when I came back after slaying Khara and other Rakshasas, so forsooth shall Bharata return to me, who have fully carried out his promise, the prosperous kingdom. See, placing the soldiers behind him and our family priest Vasistha, before Bharata, clad in bark, is coming in the company of elderly ministers with *Arghya* in his hand. Although a young man Bharata practised the hardest of vows by not enjoying the kingdom offered him by our father."

While Rama was saying this, the car, understanding his object through its presiding god, came down from the sky. Filled with surprise Bharata's subjects looked up at it. Holding Sugriva, ever intent on serving him, by the hand Rama got down from the car by the stairs of crystal pointed out by Bibhishana who went before him. Having saluted with reverence Vashistha, the family priest of [the Ikshwakus and accepting Arghya Rama embraced Bharata and Satrughna with tearful eyes and rmelt the crown of the former who, out of respect for his eldest brother, desisted from accepting the throne. And casting favourable looks on the] aged ministers whose faces were disfigured by growing beards and enquired with sweet words after their well-being.

Rama introduced very respectfully Sugriva and Bibhishana saying "He is the king of monkeys and bears. He is my great friend in calamity. And here is Pulastya's son Bibhishana who always fought before me." Thereat leaving Lakshmana Bharata first saluted Sugriva and Bibhishana. Afterwards when Bharata approached Lakshmana the latter bowed unto him. Raising him up Bharata embraced him placing his breast on his hardened by the strokes inflicted by Indrajit. Then assuming human forms at the command of Rama the commanders of the monkey army rode elephants. And temporal juice trickling down the bodies of the elephants they felt the pleasure of ascending a hill.

By the command of Rama, the king of Rakshasas got upon a car with his followers, beautifully made by his illusory power.

As the moon, beautified on account of the conjunction of Budha and Vrihaspati, ascends a cloud in the night, accompanied with lightning so Rama, with Bharata and Lakshmana, again got upon his beautiful etherial car. As assuming the first Boar-form the Lord Narayana raised up the earth, as the autumn, freed from thick clouds, displays the moon so Bharata saluted the beautiful Sita whom Rama had rescued from the great dangers of Ravana. The worshipful feet of Janaki, which were firm against the salutations of the Ten-necked demon and the head of Bharata, covered with matted locks and deprived of crown for his devotion to his eldest broter, purified each other on being united.

Going half a *Krosha* in the beautiful flowery car followed by his subjects Rama arrived at the charming garden of his capital Ayodhya adorned with a canopy made by Satrughna himself.

CANTO XIV.

Rama and Lakshmana saw their mothers in the garden miserably situated in the absence of their husband like a creeper when the tree, that supports it, is destroyed. With their vision obstructed with tears they could not behold clearly their powerful sons who had come back after killing their enemies but knew them as such by experiencing the pleasure of touching their body. As the water from the springs of the Himalaya falls down and cools the water, heated by the rays of the sun, of the Ganges who purifies the sinful and of Yamuna so their cool tears of joy removed the heat of their tears of sorrow. Touching the green wounds on the persons of Rama and Lakshmana inflicted by the weapons of the Rakshasas Koushalya and Sumitra lost respect for the favourite appellation of the Kshatriya ladies, namely "the mother of heroes." Saying "I am that inauspicious Sita who afflicted my husband," Vaidehi saluted the feet of the both the queens with equal reverence. They however, with truthful and affectionate words, consoled their daughter-in-law, saying "Rise up O child. By the purity of your character only Rama and Lakshmana have been saved from a great disaster." Then with water filling up many golden pitchers collected from many sacred shrines, and with it the tears of joy of his mothers the elderly ministers performed the preliminary part of Rama's installation. The monkeys and Rakshasas too brought water from various rivers, oceans and tanks. The torrents of water, while dropping on the head of the victorious Raghava, appeared like torrents of rain falling on the summit of the Vindhya mountain. It is a mere repitition to say that Rama, who shone exquisitely beautiful when he put on an ascetic garb before, appeared far more beautiful now when he was clad in a royal robe. Delighting the citizens with the sound of bugles, he, in the company of elderly ministers, night-rangers and monkeys, entered Ayodhya, the capital of the Raghu family, abounding in high gateways beautified with fried paddy poured down from the palaces. Lakshmana and Shatrughna fanned Rama who was seated on a car with chowries. And Bharata held the umbrella. It appeared thereat that the incarnate forms of conciliation, gifts, dissension and punishment were united. The smoke of Aguru coming out of the palace and being scattered by the wind it appeared that Rama, who had returned from the forest was, with his own hands, loosening the locks of Ayodhya who was like a woman whose husband had been away. With folded hands which were distinctly seen from the nets of the Palace Windows the women of Ayodhya saluted Sita, the wife of Raghu hero, who had been beautifully decorated by her mothers-in-law. Bearing the permanent marks of resplendent unguents offered by Anasuya, and assuming a wonderful beauty as if she had again entered into fire Sita appeared to the females as to have been considered by her husband as pure. Having offered his friends well-furnished houses, Rama, who was the mine of friendship, entered, with tearful eyes, into a house, filled with articles of worship in which only a portrait of his father remained. There with folded hands he said to Bharata's mother Kaikeyi :—

"O mother, it must be admitted that it is by thy virtue only that my father did not violate the vow of truth which yields heaven as its fruit." Saying this he removed her shame. Rama offered so many edibles to Sugriva, Bibhishana and others that though they could gather all at their merest will, they were still filled with surprise. Having duly honored Agastya and other ascetics who had assembled there to welcome him he heard from them the birth-story of his slain enemy Ravana. It mainifested greatly his own personal glory. After the great saints had departed for their respective hermitages Rama sent away Bibhishana, the king of Rakshasas and other monkey chiefs by offering them suitable presents from Janaki. After their departure they spent their days so happily that even half a month was not perceptible to them. Then he ordered the flowery car, the flower of the celestials, which he had acquired by destroying Ravana, to proceed to Kuvera, the king of Kailasha, for carrying him. Thus after the death of his father having spent fourteen years in the forest Rama assumed the reins of the Government and acted impartially towards religion, profit and desire and his three younger brothers. As sucking the breast of the six Kirtikas with His six mouths, Kartikeya, the commander-in-chief of the celestial army, pleased them so Rama, devoted to mothers, served Koushalya and others. Under the regeme of Rama shorn of avarice, the destroyer of obstacles and the remover of sorrow his subjects acquired profuse wealth, performed religious rites and obtained sons. Performing his royal duties in proper time Rama used to spend the rest of his hours happily in the company of Janaka's daughter. It so appeared that the presiding goddess of royal prosperity had been united with him in the person of Janaki. While they enjoyed immensely in the palace embellished with portraits, Rama and Sita enjoyed greater the pleasure the more they remembered their hardships in the forest of Dandaka. Then showing evident signs of conception by her countenance pale like a Sara reed and having beautiful eyes Vaidehi conduced greatly to the happiness of her Consort. Being confirmed in his belief about her conception by her blue nipples Rama, placing her on his lap in a solitary place, enquired after her desire. As ferocious animals musticate Nivara rice offered as food as Vaikhanasa maidens being united show their respective love so Janaka's daughter Sita expressed her desire to behold again the penance groves situate on the banks of Bhagirathi interspersed with Kuca grass. Rama also promised to fulfill her desire.

One day along with his followers he got on the turret of his palace to behold the delightful city of Ayodhya. Beholding the prosperous and crowded high-ways, the river Sarayu filled with boats and gardens inside the houses filled with playful citizens he experienced greatest delight. Inorder to learn the public opinion about his own character the Raghu hero of purified soul, the foremost of orators, victor of enemies and the possessor of serpentine arms, asked his secret spy Bhadra. When he pressed him much Bhadra communicated every thing to him and said :—" O god, the citizens speak highly of all thy actions. They only blame thee for having taken back Sita who had lived in the house of the Rakshasa."

As a piece of heated iron is shattered by the strokes of a massive iron club so Rama's heart was rent asunder by hearing of this charge against his wife. His mind became unsettled like a craddle being himself stupified to decide whether he would disregard the charge brought against him or forsake his own innocent wife. After thinking for a considerable time he decided that no other means would remove this blame except the forsaking of his own wife. Not to speak of the objects of enjoyment, persons, having fame for their wealth, prefer glory even to their own lives. Then Rama, who was shorn of lustre, sent for his younger brothers. When after seeing the pale countenace of their eldest brother they took their seats he communicated to them the news of the censure and said:—

"As a mirror is marked by the watery air so the pure solar dynasty has been soiled with censure through me. Consider it very well. As an elephant-chief regards the pole to which he is tied as a source of great misery so I cannot bear this blame unheared-of before, which has spread amongst my subjects like a drop of oil thrown on the agitated waves. As formerly by my sire's mandate I renounced the kingdom consisting of oceans, so for removing this censure I will forsake Sita even not caring for the hour of my son's birth. I know Janaki to be chaste, but the censure of the people has grown too much powerful for me. There is nothing which men cannot do—they consider the shadow of the earth as a spot for the spotless moon. In vain has not been my attempt to kill the Rakshasas. I have done so for subduing my enemies. A serpent, when trampled under foot, does not bite its aggressor for drinking his blood. If you think that I shall live long after removing this censure then kindly do not prevent me from doing what I have resolved."

When bent upon doing an injury to the daughter of Janaka Rama said this, none amongst the brothers could either prevent him or accept his proposal.

Casting his looks towards Lakshmana his eldest brother, truthful and illustrious in the three worlds, ordered him separately, saying "O gentle one, Sita, who is encient, has expressed her desire of seeing the penance groves. Do you under this pretext take her on a car and leave her in the hermitage of the great saint Valmiki." Lakshmana knew that Parashurama, by the command of his sire, had cut off like an enemy the head of his mother and therefore he accepted such a command of his eldest brother, for implicit submission should be paid to the orders of the elders.

Thereupon Rama's younger brother Lakshmana placed Sita, who was filled with delight on hearing of the favourable news, on a car drawn by fearless steeds and driven by the charioteer Sumantra and set out. While proceeding by charming countries Sita was filled with delight on thinking that her husband was always anxious to secure her pleasure. She did not know that Rama was no longer a Kalpa tree to her but that of sword leaves. The trembling of the right eye, which was for good deprived of the view of a desirable sight, announced on the way the future great calamity which Lakshmana had kept hidden so long. Janaki's countenance grew immediately pale with sorrow for seeing evil omens. She then with a simple mind prayed for the well-being of her most beloved Rama. Raising up her wave-like hands Janhavi prevented Lakshmana who was by the command of his brother about to leave Sita in the forest. When Sumantra stopped the horses Lakshmana helped Sita to get down from the car like a truthful person carrying out his promise and ferryied her across the river in a boat brought by Nishada. Then governing his speech with difficulty which was suppressed with tears Lakshmana expressed the order of the king as a cloud pours down hail-storms. As a flowery creeper drops on earth by the force of the wind, so Janaki, struck by this new wind, dropped down on her mother earth. Her ornaments, at that time, were scattered on all sides. Thinking "why your pious husband born in the Ikshwaku race shall forsake you for nothing" her mother Earth did not allow her to enter into her womb. While Sita was in a fainting state she did not experience the least sorrow. But on regaining her consciousness her mind was consumed with the fire of grief. The consoling words of Lakshmana were more painful to her than her unconscious state. The chaste Sita did not blame her husband the least for forsaking her without any cause but only spoke ill of her own self saying that she was ever unfortunate and sinful.

Having consoled the chaste Sita Rama's younger brother Lakshmana pointed out to her the road to Valmiki's hermitage and said "O goddess, I am dependent upon another. Pray forgive me for this cruel deed which I have committed under the order of my master." Raising him up with her hand from the ground Sita said:—"O gentle one, do thou live long. I am pleased with thee. Thou art not at all to blame. As Upendra is under Indra so thou art under thy elder brother. Communicate my salutations one by one to my mothers-in-law and tell them that they may always think of the well-being of their grandson who is in my womb. And communicate my words to the king saying "Although I proved my innocence before thee by entering into fire still thou hast forsaken me in fear of groundless censure. Is this the becoming action of the Raghu family? Thou art good by nature; I am sure thou hast not acted irresponsibly by me. This is the unbearable thunderbolt of my dreadful pristine sin. Methinks because thou didst forsake before the goddess of fortune and enter into forest with me, therefore she has been unable to bear my habitation in thy house. When the husbands of the female ascetics were formerly oppressed by the Rakshasas I gave them shelter by thy favour, how shall I seek refuge with another while thou art alive? If thy son had not been in my womb whom it is my bounden duty to protect, then I would not have kept this life rendered useless by thy separation. O Lakshmana, fixing my eyes on the sun after delivery I will carry on penances saying that I may even in my next birth obtain as my husband endued all virtues, an incarnation of Narayana and may not suffer separation from him. Manu has said that the duty of a king consists in protecting the four castes, the Brahmanas &c. and the four Ashramas of Bramacharya, &c. And although he has exiled me, he should see me considering me as an ordinary female ascetic."

When after promising that he would communicate all those words to Rama, Lakshmana disappeared from her view Rama's wife Janaki again cried bitterly like a terrified she-deer. At that time the she-peacocks desisted from dancing, the trees cast off their flowers, and the she-deer threw away the sacrificial grass they had taken up. In short sympathising with Sita's grief the entire forest wept. At that time the prime-poet Valmiki was ranging in the forest to collect sacred fuels and sacrificial grass. And following the cries he came where Sita was. He was so very compassionate by nature that he was affected by sorrow when he saw a Krouncha pierced by a hunter. This incident produced his verses. Rubbing the tears off her eyes and desisting from lamentations Maithila saluted that foremost of Munis. He too marking signs of conception blessed her saying "May you have a good son," and said "By my fore-sight I have known, that your husband Rama, his mind affected with fear of people's censure, has forsaken you. Be not grieved for it, O Vaidehi; know that you have come to your father's house, situate in another country. Rama has killed Ravana, the thorn of the world. He is truthful and shorn of pride; still I have felt anger for him for having forsaken you.

unjustly. Your illustrious father-in-law was a great friend of mine. Your father, by delivering divine instructions, shatters the worldly miseries of the pious. You are the foremost of chaste women. Why should you not then deserve my favour? By living in the company of the ascetics even the ferocious animals of this penance forest have grown quiet. You can live fearlessly in this forest; you will give birth to your son without any pain and their Jatakarma and other rites will be duly performed. By adoring your own deity on the back of the sin-destroying river Tamasa, thick set with the cottages of the Rishis your mind will be delighted. The daughters of the ascetics, fearless in speech, with collect season flowers, fruits, ingredients of worship, *Nivara* rice and please your mind who have been assailed with this new grief. By nourshing the growth of the new trees of the hermitage with pouring water according to your might you will experience parental affection before giving birth to a son."

Having said so the kind hearted ascetic Valmiki arrived in the evening at his hermitage full of quiet animals with Janaki, the object of his welcome. As Amavasya consigns the last ray of the moon whose other rays are devoured by the Pitris, to the herbs, so that foremost of ascetics entrusted Sita, who was stricken with grief, to the care of the ascetic ladies who were filled with delight at her arrival. Having duly welcomed Janaka's daughter the female ascetics, lighting up a lamp with Ingudi oil, set apart for her habitation a cottage spread with the bed of deer skin.

Having honoured duly the guests and living on wild fruits and roots for keeping up the line of her husband, Janaki, purified by bathing and clad in pure bark, spent her days in that hermitage.

On the other side discussing in his mind "Has not the king been stricken with repentance by this time?" Lakshmana, the destroyer of Indrajit, communicated to his eldest brother Rama all the incidents ending with Sita's lamentation. Hearing it Rama, like the moon of the month of Pousha pouring down dews, all on a sudden shed tears; for fear of calumny he sent away Maithili from his house, but not from his heart. Then restraining his sorrow, protecting the castes and Ashramas, and enjoying everything equally with his younger brothers Rama governed that prosperous kingdom. After he had forsaken the chaste Sita for fear of calumny the goddess of prosperity, freed from impediments and a co-wife, began to live happily on his breast. Having forsaken Janaka's daughter, Rama, the victor of Ravana, did not marry any other woman. Having heard that he had performed the horse-sacrifice with an golden image of Sita by him, she, with great difficulty, bore that sorrow.

CANTO XV.

Having forsaken Sita, Rama, the lord of the earth, began to enjoy her only whose tongue was the ocean. A Rakshasa, Lavana by name, once obstructed the sacrifice of the ascetics living on the bank of the Yamuna. Thereat they sought refuge with Rama. Finding Dasharatha's son engaged in the work of protection they did not destroy Lavana by their ascetic power, for in the absence of a protector the ascetics,[1] whose weapon is their curse, exhaust their asceticism acquired with great difficulty. Rama, the scion of the Kakustha race, promised to the Rishis to remove their hindrances, because for the protection of virtue the Lord Narayana incarnated himself as Rama on earth. The ascetics suggested to him the means of destroying Lavana. Lavana, the holder of mace, could with difficulty be conquered. He used to invite a person for fight whenever he was divested of his mace. Rama ordered Satrughna to administer to the well-being of the ascetics so that he might justify the root meaning of his name by killing the enemies. As any special injunction is capable of putting a stop to the action of general laws so any one of the Raghu family could destroy the enemies. Having accepted on his head the blessings of his eldest brother the fearless Satrughna proceeded on his car beholding the beatiful forest covered with flowers. As to signify 'Study' the prefix *adhi* follow the root *ing* so the soldiers, at the comand of Rama, follwed him for accomplishing a great work. Preceding the car the ascetics pointed out the road. Proceeding according to their directions, the effulgent Satrughna appeared like the sun in the etherial way pointed out by the Balakhilya ascetics. On his way he spent one night in the penance forest of Valmiki abounding with deer with 'heads upraised on hearing the rattle of the car-wheels. Having collected various most excellent articles by his ascetic power, that foremost of Munis, Valmiki, treated to hospitality the prince whose horses were worn out with enhaustion. As the earth gives birth to wealth and soldiers so in that night his brother's wife, who was in family way, gave birth to two sons. Being greatly delighed on hearing of the birth of sons to his eldest brother Satrughna, having saluted that foremost of ascetics with folded hands, set out on his car. Thereupon Satrughna arrived at Lavana's city Madhupaghna. At that time Kumbhinashi's son brought various animals from the forest as a tribute to the king. That Rakshasa was smoky-coloured and from his person emitted smell of fat. His hairs were twany-coloured like fire and he was encircled by Rakshasas who lived on flesh. It appeared as if the fire of funeral pyre was ranging on all sides. Seeing Lavana divested of his mace Rama's younger brother immediately attacked him, for a person who strikes his antagonist on finding a loop-hole, is always crowned with success.

Roaring at Satrughna saying "Perhaps seeing my scanty food the Providence in fear has sent you to me" that Rakshasa uprooted a huge tall tree, at him which was cut into pieces on the way by the sharpened arrows of Soumitri, and could not touch his person, the dust of the flowers only touching it. When that tree was cut into pieces the highly powerful Rakshasa Lavana hurled at Satrughua a huge piece of rock like unto a fist of Death placed elsewhere. Struck by the Indra weapon discharged by Satrughna that massive rock was shattered into atoms minuter than even sand. Then raising up his right hand the Rakshasa ran towards Satrughna like unto a portion of a hill shaken by a tornado. Then with his heart cut off by the Vishnu weapon discharged by Satrughna the Rakshasa dropped down on earth and shook her. But this removed the trembing of the Rishis living in the hermitages. The birds sat on the body of the slain enemy; and celestial flowers were poured dowu on the head of his antagonist. At that time having slain Lavana the great heroe Satrughna regarded himself the worthy younger brother of Lakshmana who had killed Indrajit. The more the ascetics, who were freed from dangers in the performance of sacrifices praised him, the greater was the bashful humiliation of his head which was upraised by his prowess. Satrughna, whose ornament was his manliness, who was shorn of desire for wordly enjoyments and whose form was gentle, made a city, by name Mathura, on the banks of Kalindi. Beholding the prosperity of the citizens under the protection of a good king people thought that the city had been peopled by the extra denizens of heaven. Ascending his palace there Satrughna experienced great delight on beholding the river Yamuna filled with Chakravakas like unto the golden tresses of the earth.

On the other side Valmiki, well-versed in mantras, the friend of both Dasharatha and Janaka, out of his love for them, performed the purificatory rites, of the both sons of Vaidehi. The impurities of the womb of one were cleansed with Kuca, and those of another with the down of the tail of a low. For this reason the Prime Poet named them Kusha and Lava. After they had passed the stage of infancy he instructed them both in the Vedas and then made them sing the Ramayana composed by his own self, the first seeds of poetry. Singing the swbet history of Rama before their mother Kusha and Lava lessened a little her sorrow consequent upon her separation from her husband. Rama's other three brothers, Bharata, Lakshmana and Satrughna, effulgent like three fires, begat two sons respectively on their wives. Having conferred the kingdoms of Mathura and Vidisa on his two sons Satrughati and Suvahu, who were well versed with the knowledge of scriptures Satrughna, who was anxious to behold his eldest brother, started for Ayodhaya.

Considering it unwise to obstruct again the asceticism of the greatest of the Rishis Valmiki, Satrughana passed over his hermitage filled with deer who were rendered motionless by the songs of the two sons of Maithili. The self-controlled Satrughana entered Ayodhya the roads of which were beautifully repaired. The citizens cast respectful looks at him for having slain Lavana. There he saw Rama, the only husband of the earth on account of his having relinquished Janaki, encircled by his courtiers. As delighted at the destruction of Kalanemi Indra received Rama so did his eldest brother receive Satrughana, who bowed unto him, for his having slain Lavana. On Rama's enquiry after his well-being he communicated every thing unto him, but he did not mention the birth of his sons for the Prime Poet asked him not to do so for he would himself return the two sons unto Rama.

One day a village Brahmin placing an infant son before the Palace gate from his lap began to sweep piteously saying—

"O Earth, slipped off the hands of king Dasharatha you were miserably plightedly. But now passing into the hands of Rama you have been visited with greater calamity."

Hearing of the cause of the Brahmana's sorrow Dasharatha's son, the protector of his subjects, was put greatly into shame for premature death had never touched the kingdom of the Ikshwakus. Consoling the sorrowful Brahmana, saying "Tarry a moment" he thought of his flowery car for vanquishing Death. Taking up his weapons Rama, the scion of the Raghu race, got upon that car and started. At that time an invisible voice from the sky was all on a sudden heard before him.

"O great king, some iniquity has prevailed amongst your subjects. Find it out and put it down and you will be successful."

Hearing those confident words and wishing to put down the transgressions of the caste he travelled on all sides on the car the flags whereof were shaken by its velocity. Then, Rama, the scion of the Ikshwaku race, saw that a person of bright eyes was practising penances with his face cast down towards a fire the smoke whereof touched the branches of the tree. When he enquired about his name and lineage that drinker of smoke said "I am a Sudra; my name is Shamvuka, I am practising penances for acquiring heaven." In order to cut off the head of that Sudra who was working the evil of his subjects on account of his not possessing the right of practising penances, Rama who was the subduer of the wicked, took up his weapou. He cut off his head from the neck, the beards of which were scorched by the scintillations of fire and which was like a lotus, the filaments whereof were destroyed by the frost. Being thus punished by the king the Sudra attained to a most excellent state which he had not acquired even by the hardest penances which were not his previlege to practise.

As after the termination of rains the autumn is united with the moon of cool rays, so the lord of the Raghu family, on his way back to Ayodhya, was united with the highly effulgent saint Agasthya. That ascetic son of Kumbha presented to Rama the valuable celestial ornaments which he had formerly obtained from the ocean as his ransom whom he had drunk up. Putting those ornaments on his arms which were shorn of the touch of Janaki's neck Rama returned to Ayodhya.

On the other hand before Rama's arrival the lifeless son of the twice-born one had revived. Regaining his son the Brahmana withdrew his charge by lauding Rama who saved his son from Death.

Thereupon for celebrating a horse-sacrifice Rama let loose a horse for grazing at large. As by pouring down rain clouds nourish crops so Sugriva, Bibhishasa and other dependant kings showered on him various articles necessary for the celebration of the same. Not only from the earth but even from luminous spheres the Rishis came from various quarters to the sacrifice of Rama, the foremost of kings and the scion of the Raghu race. The pure-souled Rishis living at her out-skirts the city of Ayodhya, having four gates, appeared like the body of Brahma which creates the worlds. Even the renuncitation of Maithili was an object of glory to him, for at the time of celebrating the sacrifice he did not take a second wife. With a golden image of Sita he had the duties of a wife performed. Then with requisite articles greater in number than what was required by the sacred prescription began the sacrifice of Rama. What more even the Rakshasas who generally obstructed sacrifices, were appointed guards there. Thereupon at Valmiki's command Maithili's sons Kusha and Lava sang about hither and thither the history of Rama known to him only. First of all it was the history of Rama; next it was composed by the Prime Poet Valmiki and thirdly the voice of Kusha and Lava was like that of the Kinnaras. Therefore there was nothing more pleasant to the audience than this. People, appreciating beauty and music, communicated to Rama the excellence of their voice and beauty. Along with his brothers Rama, with a delighted heart, began to behold them and listen to their music. Hearing their song with fixed mind and shedding tears the entire assemblage shone like a forest divested of the wind, in the morning pouring dews. All the people present in that meeting perceived strong resemblance, except in dress, between Rama and those two boys and began to look at them with winkless eyes. The people were not so much pleased with their proficiency in music as they were when they found them reluctant to accept any reward from the king. When the Emperor Rama himself enquired "Who has taught you music? What poet has composed this song ?" they mentioned the name of Valmiki. Then Rama with his younger brothers went to Valmiki and made over to him the entire kingdom except his own person. The highly merciful Rishi, saying "Kusha and Lava are your sons given birth to by Maithi" requested him to take back Sita. Thereat Rama said.

"O father, your daughter-in-law proved her innocence before me by the ordeal of fire. But my subjects, on account of the oppressions of the wicked Ravana, do not believe in her purity. If Maithili can create the confidence of the subjects in the purity of her character then I shall, at your command, take her back with the sons."

The king having promised so that foremost of ascetics, as he purifies his own self by self-restraint, brought Janaki from his hermitage through his disciples. Having finished the horse sacrifice Rama, the ornament of the Kakutstha family, collected all the citizens and sent for Valmiki. As the Rishis, with Udatha and other vowels as well as with purified Riks, adore the sun of fierce rays so the great saint, with Sita and her sons, appeared before Rama. Beholding Sita of quiescent form, clad in a silk raiment, with her eyes fixed on her feet they all regarded her as pure. Withdrawing their eyes from Sita the subjects hung down their heads like paddy plants laden with crops. Then taking his seat the foremost of ascetics said to Sita :—

"O my child, remove the misgivings of the people about your character before your husband."

Then rinsing her mouth with the sacred water offered by Valmiki's disciple Maithili pronounced her truthful vow saying "Lady earth, if I have not violated my allegiance to my husband by my speech, mind or words then give me room in your womb." On the chaste Sita saying so, immediately a circle of effulgence like unto lightning came out of the cavity of the Earth. Inside this circle of effulgence the goddess earth, having the ocean for her tongue, was distinctly seen seated on a throne upheld by the hoods of the serpents. Placing Sita, who had her eyes fixed on her husband, on her lap she returned to the nether region although repeatedly prevented by Rama to do so. The family priest Vasistha, who was cognizant of the power of the deity, pacified Rama's anger against Earth, who had taken up an arrow for compelling her to return Sita.

Having sent away his friends and the Rishis with proper honors after the termination of the sacrifice Rama transferred his love for Sita to his two sons.

At the command of Bharata's maternal uncle Yudhajit, Rama, the protector of subjects, conferred the kingdom of Sindhu with immense wealth on Bharata. Having vanquished the Gandharvas there in battle Bharata made them wield Vinas instead of weapons. Having installed his two sons by name Taksha and Pushkala he again returned to Rama.

By Rama's command Lakshmana conferred the kingdom of Karapatha on his two sons Angada and Chandraketu. Having thus distributed the kingdoms amongst their sons the kings performed the obsequial rites of their mothers who had gone to the region of their father.

Afterwards one day Death, assuming the garb of an ascetic, arrived before Rama, and said "Promise you will renounce him who will come here when we will talk in secret." Rama having agreed Yama, assuming his own form, said "By Brahma's command do thou ascend the heaven." In the meantime, Lakshmana, who was at the gate, in fear of the imprecation of Durvasa who had come there to see Rama, broke their secrecy, although he knew the former oath. Having gone to the bank of Sarayu the Yogin Lakshmana, who had violated the promise, gave up his body. His fourth part Lakshmana having gone to heaven Rama lived on earth without any tenacity like righteousness of three legs. Having placed Kusha who was like a goad to the elephant-like enemies in Kushavati and Lava who could please the pious with sweet words in Sharavati, Rama with his other brothers started for the North with fire before them. The city of Ayodhya, out of her devotion to her Lord, followed him. The monkeys and Rakshasas who knew his heart followed his foot steps which were soaked with drops of tears of the subjects big as Kadamva flowers.

Seated on the car, Rama, fond of his votaries, made the sacred Sarayu his staircase for ascending heaven in the interest of his followers. Because at that time for the creatures who were bathing in her the river Sarayu became worthy of even being crossed by the kine, so that part afterwards became the celebrated shrine of *Go-Pratara*. When Sugriva and others, who emanated from the portions of the deities, assumed their own forms Rama created another heaven for the citizens who had obtained immortality. Having thus performed the work of the gods namely the decapitation of the Ten-necked demon, and placed Bibhishana and Hanuman as two pillars of his glory on the Southern and Northern Hills, the Lord Narayana again assumed his own form, the refuge of all the worlds.

CANTO XVI.

Rama having obtained emancipation Lava and six other Raghu heroes conferred on Kusha, who was the eldest and the most accomplished, all the most excellent properties for brotherliness was a hereditary quality in their family. Although they grew powerful by constructing bridges, encouraging husbandry, protecting kine and procuring elephants still they did not go beyond their respective boundaries as the ocean does not transgress its continent. The families of

Kusha, Lava and others the generous sons of Rama and other incarnations of the four-armed Narayana were divided into eight branches like unto those of the eight elephants of the quarters sprung from the Sama Veda.

Once on a time when the wick of the lamp was motionless, and all the inmates of the bed-room were fast asleep Kusha awoke all on a sudden and saw the unforeseen figure of a woman who was dressed like one whose husband was away. Having uttered the word *Jaya* before Kusha, who was powerful like Indra, a victor of enemies and whose wealth was enjoyed by the pious, the charming woman stood with folded hands. Then raising up the upper part of his body the great bowman Kusha, the grandson of Dasharatha, was filled with surprise on seeing the beautiful form of a woman entering into the room locked up like unto a reflection in the mirror and said :—

"O fair one, how have you entered this room which has been locked up. It seems you are not endued with the power of Yoga and your appearance is pale like a lotus assailed with frost. Who are you and whose wife? Why have you come to me in the dead of night? The mental faculties of the self-controlled descendants of the Raghu family are always averse to others' wives. Considering this, reply fearlessly to my questions." Thereat that well-dressed and ault-less lady replied.

"O king, know me as the presiding goddess of that lordless city of Ayodhya the virtuous citizens of which your father had taken away with him at the time of his departure for his own region. Formerly I excelled even the prosperous city of Alaka filled with festivities under the regeme of the king of celestials. But even inspite of the existence of such an illustrious descendant of the solar dynasty, as yourself, I have come by such a pitiable situation. As the period of junction is situated when the sun sets and the clouds are dispersed by a strong wind, so is my condition for hundreds of palaces have become unworthy of habitation, their walls dismantled and houses broken in the absence of occupiers. Formerly in the depth of night unchaste women, with Nupuras ringing on their feet, used to wend the high ways; now jackals are moving about with hideous yells in search of flesh. Formerly the water of the tanks moved by the hands of women while sporting there used to imitate the sound of Mridanga and now that clear water is being agitated by the horns of wild buffaloes. Their houses being broken the sportive peacocks are lying on the trees. They no longer dance now for want of the music of Mridanga. And being consumed by the forest-fire the gardens have come by the condition of the peacocks. The stairs on which formerly the women used to place their feet dyed with red lac are now being printed with the foot-prints of the tigers marked with the blood of the deer killed immediately.

The painted figures of the elephants in the forest of lotuses are now bearing the marks of the claws of the angry lions; the sloughs of the serpents are covering the breasts of the figures of the women painted on the pillars the colour of which has faded away in time. The white colour of the houses has grown pale in time and grass has grown over them. The rays of the moon like unto pearls are not reflected on them in the night. The creepers of my gardens which the sportive women used to bend with great care for plucking flowers are being scattered by the wild monkeys and other animals. No longer the flame of the lamps goes out through my windows in the night, nor are they adorned with the beautiful faces of the women during the day. In time the sacred smoke of Aguru and sandal has disappeared and the houses have been covered with the cob-webs of creepers. Alas! on seeing the condition of the river Saraju now my mind becomes greatly afflicted. Her banks are shorn of food offerings. Her streams no longer carry the scented ingredients of bathing and the Vetasa groves on her bank are not resorted to by men. Therefore O king, as your father having cast off the human body undertaken by him for his own works, has assumed again the form of Vishnu so leaving this city of Kushavati go to your ancestral city of Ayodhya."

Saying 'so be it' the Raghu hero Kusha delightedly accepted her proposal and that beautiful damsel too, with a smiling countenance, disappeared therefrom. The next morning the king communicated that wonderful incident to the Brahmanas assembled in his court. Hearing of it and learning that the capital of his family had accepted Kusha as his lord the Brahmanas welcomed him with their blessings. Then having left his own city Kushavati in charge of the Brahmanas conversant with the Vedas the Emperor Kusha, on an auspicious day, with the ladies of his seraglio and encircled by his soldiers, set out for Ayodhya like unto the wind preceding the clouds. While the soldiers marched the flags imitated the beauty of the gardens, the elephants that of pleasure hills and the cars that of huge palaces. It appeared as if the city was going. Having the white umbrellas for their reflections the soldiers, proceeding towards Ayodhya at the command of Kusha, appeared like the ocean rising up to the bank at the advent of the moon. As if unable to bear the obstruction of the soldiers when Kusha set out the goddess Earth ascended the etherial region in the shape of dust. A portion of the army were busy with leaving the city of Kushavati, another detachment were busy with encamping before and the third proceded on their way. It appeared therefore that all the divisions were united there. With the temporal juice of the infuriated elephants and the strokes of the hoofs of the horses belonging to the Emperor Kusha the dust was converted into mud and the latter was again converted into dust. The soldiers, being scattered while searching the roads on the levelled surface of the mount Vindhya, set up a terrible uproar resounding the caves thereof like the river Reva. Going over the red chalk and other minerals of the mountains the wheels of the cars were dyed therewith and their rattle was mixed with the sound of bugles. In this wise marking presents offered by the Pulindas the king Kusha crossed the mount Vindhya. While at the sacred shrine of the Vindhya he was crossing the river Ganges flowing towards the west with a bridge of elephants the swans, flying in the sky, served for the time being for his chowries, their wings moving without any care. Then the king Kusha saluted the sacred water of the Ganges which was the source of heaven to his ancestors who were reduced to ashes by the anger of Kapila and was shaken by the movements of boats. Thus traversing the roads for a few days he at last arrived at the bank of the river Sarayu and observed the sacrificial stakes by hundreds, erected on the altars, by the Raghu kings who were constantly engaged in sacrifices. Then the extremity wind of his ancestral capital, cooled by its coming in contact with the waves of Sarayu, shaking the branches of the trees went forward to welcome Kusha ircled by soldiers worn out with fatigue of travel.

Thereupon the powerful king, the victor of enemies and the friend of the citizens, encamped, at the boundary of the city of Ayodhya, his soldiers with the hoisting of flying banners. As the cloud with the downpour of rain, vivifies the earth stricken with the rays of the sun, so the artists, engaged by their master, with various ingredients laid out anew the city which was so miserably plighted. Then with the help of persons conversant in the knowledge of adoring Vastu, the presiding deity of the house, the Raghu hero Kusha offered adoration at the spacious temples with sacrifices of beasts. As a lustful person gains the heart of his sweet heart with advances of love so the king Kusha, entering the palace, honored his ministers with offering them houses according to their ranks. With shops filled with various commodities for sale, with horses in the stable and elephants tied to the stakes the city appeared perfectly beautiful. Residing in Ayodhya the capital of the Raghus, rendered again as beautiful as before, Maithili's son Kusha did not aspire after the city of the king of gods or after that of Kuvera. Thereupon set in summer as if for making the beloved wives of Kusha to put on robes set with pearls, to bear necklaces on their breasts and for instructing them to make decorations. When the sun approached nearer from the quarter presided over by Agasthya the North discharged the snowy water of the Himalaya like the delightful cool water. At that time the heat of the day was increased and the night was shortened. So they both appeared like two penitent wives separated from their husband by the quarrels of love. Day by day water of the tanks went down the stairs covered with mosses and the stalks of lotuses rose above water. By and by water, up to the waist of women, was left in the tanks. Unfolding themselves in the evening the Mallika flowers spread fragrance on all sides of the forest. Going to every flower the black-bees were as if counting their number by their hummings. The filaments of Sirisha flowers being stuck on the cheeks of the women filled with perspiration and cut with nails, they did not drop down on earth, although displaced from the ears. Lying on the stone-floors of their houses washed with water and besmeared with sandal the rich people began to ward off the heat of the sun. In the end of the spring, the lustful movements of the hairs of women loosened after bathing, scented with incense, and covered with Mallika flowers, roused the weak Cupid. The twany-coloured blossoms of the Arjuna flowers appeared like the broken bow of the god of love who was reduced to ashes by the fiery anger of Hara. Presenting Sahakara flowers of sweet scent, the fragrant old Siddha and new Patali flowers as well as other charming objects the summer, as if, made himself freed from the charge of spreading painful heat from the pleasure-seeking persons. In this painful season two things were greatly liked by people the moon enveloped with rays capable of removing the distresses of heat and the feet of the prosperous king Kusha capable of removing the misery of people. The king Kusha felt a desire of sporting with his wives in the waters of Sarayu abounding in ganders made restive by her waves and having her bank filled with blossoming creepers. That king, powerful like Vishnu, had a tent pitched on her bank and crocodiles and other ferocious acquatic animals removed by fishermen. He then, as becoming his might and wealth, began to sport in the water. With the sound of armlets, touching one another, of his wives as well as that of the Nupuras when they got down from the bank by the stairs the swans of the river Sarayu were greatly agitated. While seated on a boat the Emperor was witnessing the sport of the women with throwing water at one another he spoke to the two women by his sides who were fanning him with chowries.

" Look with the unguents of hundreds of ladies of my seraglio the stream, of the river Sarayu, is appearing like an evening, assuming various hues by means of clouds. The waters, shaken by the boat, are removing the collyrium of their eyes and imparting in its stead, inebriete glances. Although they are unable to bear the weight of their persons on account of their heavy waists and breasts still out of attachment they are with difficultly swimming with their arms adorned with Keywers. These ear-decorations of Sirisha flowers, made by these women sporting in the water, dropping off their ears, are deceiving the fishes fond of mosses. The pear-like drops of water falling on the breasts of these women engaged in throwing up water it is appearing as if chains of pearls are dropping. The objects imitating their form and beauty have come near them. The eddies are like their deep navels, the waves are like the gestures of their eye-brows and the pairs of Chakravakas are like their breasts. The sound of water like Mridangas struck by these women and welcomed by the peacocks with their notes is filling our ears. The cloth being wetted and tied on their waists the pores of the ornaments, filled up with water and disappearing like stars with the rise of the moon, have become silent. They are throwing water at their friends and who are, in return, throwing the same on their faces. Drops of water, rendered bright with Kumkuma powder, are coming down from their straight hairs. Although their tresses have been loosened and their pearl ornaments have been slackened still their beauty has not suffered deterioration."

As taking up lotuses on his shoulder a wild elephant sports with she-elephants so getting down from the boat Kusha began to sport with them. United with that effulgent king the women appeared greatly beautiful. Pearl is of itself pleasing to the eye. It indeed looks wonderfully beautiful when it is united with the shining Indra-neela stone. The women of large eyes sprinkling the king with water mixed with Kumkuma he looked like a mountain-chief besmeared with red chalk. When he bathed with the beautiful ladies of his seraglio in the river Sarayu he looked like the king of gods sporting in the Mandakini in the company of Apsaras. Rama gave Kusha along with the kingdom the celestial ornament which he had obtained from Agastya. While he sported in the water that Jaitra ornament dropped there against his knowledge. When after performing that desirable ablution he arrived at the tent with those women he found, before rubbing, his arm divested of that celestial ornament. That ornament was the master of victory and used by his father. And therefore he could not bear its loss and not out of avarice. To that wise, rich and considerate king flowery and jewelled ornaments were of equal value. The king Kusha immediately ordered fishermen, expert in diving into the water of the river, to find it out. They tried their best; but being unsuccessful and filled with sorrow they said :—

"O lord, we have tried our best but have not been able to find out your jewelled ornament thrown into water. Forsooth the Naga Kumuda, living in the river, has taken it out of avarice."

Thereupon with his eyes reddened in anger, the great bowman Kusha, stringing his bow, arrived at the bank of the lake and took up the Garuda weapon for killing the serpent. As soon as the arrow was shot the lake was agitated. And as if striking the bank with its hand, the wave, like an elephant thrown into a pit, began to roar terribly. As the Kalpa tree rose with Lakshmi from the ocean when it was churned so the king of Nagas, with a beautiful maiden, came out of the lake the acquatic animals whereof were greatly assailed. Beholding the king of serpents who had arrived there for returning the ornament the king withdrew his arrow, for the anger of the pious does not last long against the humiliated persons seeking their shelter. Then bowing down his head the Naga Kumuda saluted Kusha, the goad of elephant-like enemies and the son of Rama, the king of the three worlds, and said :—

"I know you as the another form in the shape of a son of the Lord Narayana, who had assumed a human form for relieving the earth of her burden. How can I then obstruct your pleasure? This maiden, fickle on account of her youth, was playing with balls. While she looked up to mark them she saw your ornament dropping in the lake like a star from the sky and took it up. Let this jem of an ornament, O king, be united with thy strong arm, extending to the knees, marked with bow-strings and like unto a shelter for protecting the world. O Scion of the Raghu race, now my prayer before you is that you may be pleased to permit this my youngest sister Kumudvati to expatiate her sin by serving your feet for ever."

When Kumuda returned the ornament after saying

this Kusha, pleased, replied :—" O king of serpents, you are an honorable friend of mine, so I cannot disregard your prayer."

Afterwards in the company of his friends the Naga-chief Kumuda duly united Kumudvati, the ornament of both the races, with Kusha. When the king, for securing a helpmate in religious practices, accepted her hand before the flaming fire all the quarters were filled with the sound of bugles and a wonderful shower of sweet-scented flowers fell there. In this way the Naga-chief Kumuda obtained Kusha begotten on Maithili by the foremost of kings, Rama, the preceptor of the three worlds, as his friend. And Kusha too secured Kumuda, the fifth son of Takshaka, as his friend. The first obtained freedom from the fear of Garuda, the destroyer of his father and the latter happily governed the earth divested of the fear of serpents.

CANTO XVII.

As from the third part of the night intellect obtains delight so Kumudvati obtained as her son the Kakutstha prince *Atithi*. As the sun of incomparable effulgence lights up both the north and the south so Atithi of incomparable beauty purified both the families of his father and mother Then his sire, the foremost of all those conversant in the worldly object, first instructed his son in all the branches of learning and afterwards had him married with the daughters of the kings. Having obtained that powerful and self-controlled son the heroic, self-controlled king Kusha regarded himself fortunate and helpful. Then as becoming his family, he, for helping the king of celestials, killed an invincible Daitya and was himself also slain by him. As a lily follows the moon affording delight to her, so Kumudvati, sister of the Naga king Kumuda, followed him. One of them occupied with the king of heaven the half of his throne and the other shared Parijata with Sachi. Then remembering the last mandate of the king before he set out for the battle the elderly ministers thought of installing his son Atithi on the throne. For his installation the ministers had a new hall erected by the artists supported by four pillars and containing an elevated altar. The subjects brought golden pitchers filled with sacred water before the king Atithi who was seated on an auspicious altar in that Hall. With the calm and deep sound of the bugles at the gate it was ascertained that his auspiciousness would be permanent in his generation. With grass, barley seeds, bark of fig-tree and new leaves the elderly kinsmen performed the rite of Neerajana. First of all reciting the mantrams of the Atharva Veda his priests and other Brahmanas began the ceremony of installation. The water, pouring with a sound on his head appeared like the stream of the Ganges falling on the head of the destroyer of Tripura. As when the clouds appear the Chatakas welcome them so the panegyrists sang his glories at the time of installation. After the termination of the installation ceremony he gave profuse wealth to the priests so that their sacrifices might be celebrated with sufficient presents. The blessings which they delightedly showered on the Emperor were the outcome of his pristine virtue. He set the prisoners at liberty, forgave the culprits who were to have been hanged, set free the beasts of burden and stopped the milching of the kine. By his command the Suka and other birds that were in the cage were set free and fled away at their pleasure.

Thereupon for the purpose of dressing, the king sat, in another room, on a most excellent throne covered with a sheet of ivory. Washing their hands with water the attendants decorated, with scents and garlands, the dried hairs of Athiti. On the pearl chains with which his hairs were tied they put brilliant rubies. Having rubbed his body with sandal scented with musk they put on marks of *Gorochana*. Adorned with all the ornaments and clad in a silk raiment marked with the emblems of swans the king, bearing garlands, looked exquisitely beautiful like the bride-groom of the goddess of regal prosperity. While Atithi saw his decorations in a gold mounted mirror his reflection there looked beautiful like that of the Kalpa tree reflected on the Meru at the time of the rising of the sun. Then exclaiming his victory his attendants, carrying chowries, umbrellas and other parapharnalia of royalty, moved on around him. He then entered the Assembly Hall like unto that of the celestials and sat on the beautiful ancestral throne beautified with a canopy which was marked with the lines of the crown jems of tributary kings. When he sat on the throne that spacious hall, resembling the house of Srivatsa, looked like the breast of Keshava bearing the mystic mark of Srivatsa and adorned with the Kaustava jem. Atithi was installed as heir apparent in his boyhood and therefore early gained the empire. He thereat looked like the full-moon with the immediate termination of lunar curves. His attendants considered the sweet-speeched Emperor, of smiling countenance, as a reservoir of trust. Riding on an elephant powerful like Airavata, Atithi, powerful like Indra himself, converted the city, adorned with Kalpa-tree-like flags, into heaven itself. The umbrella, of pure lustre, which was held over his head, removed the sorrow of the world consequent upon the absence of the late king. The flame of fire issues after smoke; with the rise of the sun its rays appear. But transgressing this natural virtue of luminous bodies, Atithi appeared with all the virtues and accomplishments aggregated. As an autumnal night, with the eye of a delightful star, sees the Dhruva so the beautiful damsels of the city, with eyes expanded with joy, began to look at Atithi. Throned as images in the spacious temple of Ayodya all the deities engaged in meditating on the well-being of Atithi who was worthy of that favour. Before the altar, which was wetted with the water of installation, was dried, the ocean of his power went to the end of the bank. When the counsels of the family priests Vasistha, and arrow of the bow-man, Atithi, were united what was there which was difficult of being accomplished. Encircled by pious friends, he every day, casting off idleness, used to look after all affairs so that without doubt he might ascertain proper persons of favour. Whenever pleasing him with the accomplishment of an object the dependants prayed for rewards they got riches beyond their expectations. By the administration of the previous king the subjects had grown prosperous like a river in the month of Sravana; but now they grew immensely rich like that of Bhadra. Whatever he said never proved otherwise. He never took back whatever he gave away. This rule was violated only in the case of uprooting the enemies and placing them again in their respective positions. Youth, beauty and wealth—any of these three is sufficient to create pride. But all these three were united in him and still he was not puffed up with pride. His subjects grew daily attached to him. Although he was placed newly on the throne still he became invincible like a firmly rooted tree. External enemies are not eternal for they live at a distance and therefore first of all he conquered the internal enemies, the six passions.

The goddess of prosperity, fickle by nature, became constant to that king of pleasing countenance like unto the line of gold on a testing stone. Conduct, shorn of bravery, is the characteristic of cowardice and continual display of bravery is the nature of ferocious animals; considering this Atithi used to do works by both the means. As the sun, after the rains, spreads its rays everywhere so he collected all informations of his kingdom through emissaries. He used to perform duties alloted to the kings both in the day and night as followed by Manu, and other kings. He never neglected them. He used to consult daily his leading ministers. Although discussed continually his secret counsels never saw the wind. Although he used to sleep in proper time still he kept information of his own and foreign countries through secret spies. Thus he was wide awake both day and night. Atithi used himself to besiege enemies' citadels, but his own fortresses were invincible, for a lion, the killer of elephants, does not lie in the cave out of fear. His good works used to pass secretly through deliberations and discussions like the Shali rice. As when the ocean of salt-water rises it does not go by a wrong way but goes to the mouth of the river so though he grew immensely prosperous he never wended evil ways. He was always capable of allaying immediately the displeasure of his subjects but he never gave an opportunity for the same. Although very powerful he used to fight with those whom he could defeat, for a forest-fire, when it is helped by the wind, does not go to the water. He never obstructed religion with desire or profit or the latter two with the former; nor did he obstruct profit with desire, nor desire with profit. In fact, he was equally inclined to all these three. There is no use of making friendship with poor men. And it is dangerous to make friends with rich people. He therefore contracted friendship with middle class people. When comparing his own strength with that of the enemies he found his own sufficient he started for battle. Otherwise he desisted from the attempt. Knowing that every body seeks protection when the treasury is full he used to collect money, for the Chatakas seek the clouds surcharged with water. First throwing obstacles in the way of the enemies, he himself engaged in war. Hiding his own defects he took advantage] of enemies' loopholes and killed them. He never considered, different from his own person, the soldiers trained up in the use of arms by the quiet king Kusha. Like unto the jem on the head of a serpent the enemies could not draw his three-fold power of strength, *mantrams* and good counsels. But as a load-stone draws iron so he used to rob the three-fold power of his enemies. The merchants used to move about in the rivers of their own accord as if in tanks, in the forests as if in gardens and on mountains as if in their own houses. Atithi used to protect asceticism from obstacles and wealth from robbers. And in its stead the ascetics living in the hermitages and the four orders used to confer on him one-sixth of their produces. As he used to protect the earth so she too gave him jems out of mines, corns from fields and elephants from forests. He was clever enough to employ six-fold qualities and armies on their proper objects. Thus gradually employing the four means of regal policy he was crowned with success in all his undertakings. The goddess of victory, who always follows the heroes, used to go to him engaged in righteous warfare like an unchaste woman athough he knew unfair warfare.

As the ordinary elephants, depressed by the smell of temporal juice of other elephants, do not fight with them so his enemies, depressed by his prowess, hardly fought with him. The moon after attaining the highest increase wanes; the ocean rising up to the highest point recedes; but he, although highly prosperous like the both, never knew deterioration. As the clouds are filled with water after going to the ocean, so poor people, beggars and pious men, going to that king, were loaded with riches. He always performed praise-worthy deeds but felt bashfulness when any one praised him. Still his glory, who never liked flattery, spread on all sides. Like the rising sun Atithi used to destroy the sin of his subjects by conducting them into his presence. And he used to destroy their ignorance by instructing them in the reality of things. Thus did he bring the subjects under his control.

The rays of the moon cannot touch the lotus and those of the sun cannot touch the lily, but the virtues of that accomplished king went even to his enemies. The deception practised by the Emperor on his enemies when he set out on an expedition of conquest of celebrating a horse-sacrifice was considered moral. As Indra is the king of gods, so Atithi, wending good ways as sanctioned by the scriptures, became the Lord Paramount of all the kings by his power. By the equilibrium of qualities, he became the fifth guardian deity, the sixth element, and seventh boundary mountain. As the celestials carry out the commands of Indra so the kings, leaving their umbrellas at a distance, used to carry out his mandate with uncovered heads. With so profuse presents did he worship the priests in the horse-sacrifice that his name became equally celebrated with that of Kuvera. The king of gods used to pour rain, Death used to suppress disease and Varuna made the rivers fordable for the easy passage of the boats. Thus did the guardian deities do his works like those living under his protection.

CANTO XVIII.

Atithi, the victor of enemies, begat on the daughter of Arthapati, the king of Nishadas, a son by named

Nishadha who was strong like the mount Nishadha. As people are filled with joy on seeing ripening paddy in the rains so determining that he would hand over the government to the youthful and powerful Nishada he attained to great delight. Having enjoyed the objects of the world for a long time and made over the government to his own son, Kumuda's son Atithi repaired to heaven acquired by his pure deeds. The incomparable heroe Nishadha reigned supreme over the earth containing oceans. His eyes were expansive like lotus petals, his mind was deep like the ocean and his arms were long like the bolts of the city.

After his demise his son Nala, effulgent like fire, obtained the kingdom. As an elephent breaks down the forest of reeds so the lotus-eyed Nala grinded his enemies. The king, whose glories were sung by the sky-rangers, the Gandharvas and others, obtained a son by name Nabha who was blue-hued like the sky. Like the downpours of the month of Shravana he became a favourite of the subjects. Having conferred the kingdom of Ayodhya on his worthy son the pious king Nala repaired to the forest in his old age and lived there in the company of the deer. He begat a son by Name Pundarika, unconquerable to the kings, like unto Pudarika amongst the elephants of the quarters. Having left the kingdom in the hands of his forgiving son Kshemadhanwa, ever engaged in the well-being of the subjects, Pundarika, of sure aim, repaired to forest for practising penances.

Kshemadhanwa obtained a god-like son who always went before the commanders in battle. His other name Devanika was also celebrated in heaven. As Keshemadhanwa was greatly happy in obtaining his son Devanika who was always ready to serve his father so the son too was highly pleased with the affection of his sire.

Having entrusted the charge of his subjects to the care of his son resembling his own self Kshemandhanwa repaired to the region of the celestials. By his sauvity of manners Ahinagu, the self-controlled son of Devanika, became not only a favourite of his own people but even of his enemies; for by sweet words even excited deer are brought under control.

Ahinagu, the highly powerful son of Devanika, conquered the entire world. He never mixed in bad company in his youth and always abstained from the corrupt habits of drinking, gambling &c. After his father Devanika, the clever Ahinagu, who was an expert in studying mankind, became the master of the four quarters by the four-fold means of conciliation &c., like the Prime Purusha Vishnu incarnate in four parts.

After the demise of Ahinagu his son Parijatra obtained the throne. In prosperity he excelled the Kula mountain Parijatra. Parijatra begat a son, liberal-minded and of a spacious breast, whose name was Shila. He conquered his enemies with arrows and felt himself abashed when any one lauded him.

Having installed the wise Shila as the heir-apparent the blameless king Parijatra enjoyed pleasure, for kings, for various pressing works, can never enjoy pleasures like a prisoner. As if growing jealous on seeing the love of women for Shila, who was not satiated with pleasures of life and who was a favourite to] women for his beauty, decrepitude soon overtook him. Shila begat a son by name Unnabha who was well-known, the foremost of all kings and deep-navelled like the lotus-navelled deity. After him Unnabha's son Vajra-nabha, who weilded thunder-bolt in battle, became the king of the Earth who paid him tribute in diamonds. After the departure of Vajranabha to heaven by his piety, the earth, with oceans, began to serve his son Sankhana with presents of jems produed from the mines. After his demise his son, effulgent like the sun and beautiful like Aswin, obtained the ancestral throne. Encamping soldiers and horses on the bank of the ocean he became celebrated on earth by the name of Vyushi-tashwa. He begat a son by name Vishwasaha the friend of the universe who, by worshipping the Lord of the universe, was capable of govering the entire world. As fire, the friend of the wind, becomes unbearable unto the trees, so Vishwasaha, well-versed in polity, having obtained a son by name Hiranya-nabha, a portion incarnate of Narayana, became invincible unto his enemies. Desirous of enjoying eternal happiness in his old age, Vishwasaha, the lord of subjects, who was freed from the debt to his ancestors, installed the long-armed Hiranyanabha on the throne and put on bark. Hiranyanabha, the scion of the solar dynasty, the lord of Ayodhya and the drinker of Soma juice, begat a son by name Koushalya, pleasant to the eyes like unto the second moon.

Koushalya whose fame reached even the Assemblage of Brahma, engaged his son Brahmishtha, who was devoted to Brahma, in the porotection of the subjects and was himself immersed in Para Brahma. The king Brahmistha, the ornament of his family, governing the earth without a hitch. His subjects enjoyed bliss for a long time with eyes full of tears of joy. His son Putra, whose soul was purified by serving the elders, who took after Narayana and was lotus-eyed, made his sire Brahmistha the foremost of those having sons. Thinking that the prestige of his family would be sustained by his son, Brahmistha, who had abstained from worldly pleasures, the future friend of the king of gods, bathed at the sacred shrine of Tripushkara and attained to the dignity of a celestial.

On the full-moon day the queen of the king Putra gave birth to a son, more effulgent than the Pushparaga jem, by the name of Pushya. When he appeared like the Pushya star his subjects grew highly prosperous. Having transferred the earth to his son, the Emperor Putra, afraid of the next birth, received initiation from Jaimini, conversant with the nature of Brahman. And learning the practice of

Yoga from him the great Yogin attained to emancipation. Then Dhruvasandhi, the son of the pious king Pushya, became the lord of the earth. That truthful king never broke treaties with submissive kings. His son Sudarshana, beautiful like the moon of the first day of lunar fortnight, having eyes like those of a deer, became charming even in his infancy. While a-hunting king Dhruvasandhi was killed by a lion. Seeing the wretched condition of the lord-less poor subjects the ministers unanimously installed the infant son of the king on the throne of Ayodhya. The Raghu family, governed by that boy king, looked beautiful like the sky adorned with the new moon, like a forest inhabited by one lion and water bedecked with lotuses. The crowned boy king gradually became powerful like his father. The entire population of Ayodhya considered it so. It is seen, that a piece of cloud of the size of a span, by the help of the preceding wind, enshrouds the entire welkin. When clad in a lustrous royal robe he passed by high-ways on the back of an elephant the elephant-keepers used to hold him and the subjects used to regard him with respect like a father for though a boy of six years he was still their king. Though he could not fully cover his father's throne when he sat on it but it was filled with the golden lustre of his person. Lowering their crowns the kings used to salute his feet dyed with red arsenic, which, hanging a little down from the throne, could not touch the golden foot stool. As it is not improper to call a ruby, of deep violet colour though it has a bluish tint so the appellation of Emperor was not unbecoming of that boy-king. The command, of the mouth of that boy-king, which was decorated with curling locks shaken by the wind of the chowries, suffered no violation up to the bank of the ocean. Bearing the mark of royality on his fore-head adorned with gold that king of a smiling countenance, deprived the beautiful faces of the wives of his enemies, of their paintings. That king, more tender than a Shirisha flower, used to feel pain even in putting on ornaments; but by his prowess he did not experience the least pain in carrying the heavy burden of the earth. Before learning the business of state he had studied Polity by the help of elderly ministers. Not finding an opportunity to sit on the unspacious breast of Sudarshana and waiting for the same for his advanced youth, goddess of prosperity, as if out of shame, embraced him in the shape of the shade of umbrella. The signs of bow-strings were not printed on his arms till then, the sword did not touch his fist still that arm protected the earth. Not only his body was developed in time, but the hereditary qualities of generosity, bravery etc., so liked by people, which lay latent in him, were also developed. Sudarshana, a favourite to his elders, had mastered all the branches of learning in his former birth and now recollecting them he at once regained that learning, the source of the attainment of three objects as well as his paternal nature. While learning the use of arms and studying he used to tie up his hairs. Spreading forward the fore part of his body and bending a little his left thigh he drew his bow and looked exquisitely beautiful. Then he attained his youth, the only place of amusement, which is an object of attachment like honey pleasing to the eyes of lustful women, like the flowers of the tree of Cupid and which is like the natural ornaments for all the limbs. With a view that he might have a good son the ministers brought a princess, more beautiful than a photo shown by a female agent. Becoming the wife of the prince that youthful princess became a co-wife with the goddess of prosperity.

CANTO XIX.

Having installed his son Agnivarna, effulgent like fire, on his own throne, the self-controlled king Sudarshana, the foremost of those conversant in Sastras, repaired to the Naimisha forest in his old age. Forgetting the tank of his house through sacred water, his royal bed through Kuca reed, and Palace through the thatched cottage he practised there desire-less penances. Agnivarna did not experience the least inconvenience in governing his kingdom for having uprooted the enemies by the strength of his own arms his father consigned the earth to him duly for his enjoyment. He did not leave any thorn of an enemy to be rooted out. Having governed the kingdom for a few years the lustful Agnivarna left it entirely in the hands of his ministers and became mad after women. Pleasure-parties held in his Palace filled with the sound of Mridangas and women clouded even the great festivities of his ancestors. He could not spend a moment without any object of sense. Day and night he lived in the inner apartment and never thought of subjects who came to interview him. Even if he, at the request of his ministers, allowed his subjects to see him it was only his feet which they could behold through the holes of the windows. His dependants only saluted his dyed feet like unto lotuses touched by the new rays of the sun. When the lustful Agnivarna used to sport in the water of the tanks, the lotuses thereof were agitated by the rising breasts of the youthful damsels. There was a secret house built in that tank where he used to sport with women. The collyrium of the eyes and the paintings of lips of those women on being washed by water they looked whitish. At that time the natural beauty of their face was perceptible at which the king was more tempted. As an elephant, in the company of his female mate, devours lilies so he, in the company of women, used to drink wine, in a drinking site, sweet-scented with the smell of mango blossoms. The women liked to drink secretly the wine of his mouth; he too, equally anxious, used to drink the wine of mouth offered by them. Vina emitting sweet music and sweet-speeched women used always to occupy his lap. He never allowed it to remain empty. With his body and armlets shaking at the time of playing on the musical instruments, the king Agnivarna, an expert in the science of music, used to charm the dancing girls so much that failing to follow the new method they felt shame before the teacher seated by them. After the termination of dancing he, airing their beautiful faces with breaths, the paintings whereof were washed off with drops of perspiration, used to kiss them. At that time he used to think himself more powerful than the lord of Alaka, the city of immortals. While in the company of that king who, unsolicited, used to enjoy the objects of pleasure, his favourite women showed him half of the same and kept hidden another half. Deceiving the women he used to receive from them rebukes in the shape of the pointing of finger, contraction of eye-brows and the binding with Mekhalas. In the night of sexual intercourse when his favourite women used to come on turns he, hiding himself in the back of one of them, though within the knowledge of the female emissary, used to hear her lamentations, the outcome of the fear of separation. When he felt desire for the dancing girls in the presence of his wives he used to paint their bodies with perspiring fingers and bear himself up with great difficulty. Being jealous of the women who were proud of the king's love aud worked up with passion the queens too, casting off anger, used to invite the king and have their lust satisfied. When Agnivarna used to come in the morning they, finding marks of other women on his body, felt anger and he too propitiated them with folded hands. And again showing laxity of love he used to repent again. When the king mentioned the name of another wife in a dream his other wives expressed their anger by overturning bed sheets, shedding tears and breaking bracelets. Coming to the groves of creepers adorned with flowery beds in the company of the procuress pointing out the way he, trembling in fear of his wives, used to hold sexual intercourse with the maid servants. Whenever he mentioned the name of one of his lady loves his wife said :—"O lustful man, I have got the name of your dearest lady, now I wish to have her good fortune. My mind has grown anxious for it." When the lustful Agnivarna got up from his bed it showed many marks of sexual intercourse. Some part was covered with the powder of Kumkuma, some part was filled with bees, some part was covered with torn waist-chains and somewhere was dyed with red arsenic. He used to dye the feet of his women with his own hands; but when his eyes were fixed on their waist with loosened clothes or on their buttocks he could not concentrate his attention. When newly married damsels used to turn back their mouths when kissing or withdraw their tongues their attempts became like fuels to the fire of his passion. When seeing the marks of sexual intercourse in the mirror he used to laugh behind them his wives bent their bashful heads on the smiling reflections. When after the termination of the night the king attempted to leave the bed his wives, throwing their tender arms round his neck, and putting down his feet with their fingers, used to pray for kisses. Beholding his royal dress, putting the beauty of Indra even into shade, the youthful Agnivarna did not experience that delight which he felt on marking distinctly the signs of sexual intercourse in the mirror. When he attempted to leave their side on the pretext of attending to a friend's business, his favourites said "O cheat! I have come to know your pretext of flying away" and held him by the hairs. Worn out with the fatigue of sexual intercourse the women, embracing him, used to lie down on his breast the sandal paste whereof was removed by the pressure of their rising breasts. Hearing from their secret emissary that another woman was ranging secretly in the night for having sexual pleasure his wives came to him and said "O lustful man, where will you go in this dark night and spend it there." Saying so they used to stop him. Feeling the pleasure of the embraces of women pleasant like the rays of the moon Agnivarna used to keep up nights and sleep during the day; so he imitated the nature of the moon. The lips of the songstresses were cut with his teeth and their thighs with his nails. So feeling pain either in playing on the flute or on the Vina they used to cast frowning looks at him which were objects of temptation to him. Showing secretly before the dancing girls three forms of dancing he used to vie with expert teachers before his friends. Adorning his limbs with Kutaja and Arjuna flowers and painting his body with the filaments of Kadamva flowers in the rains he used to pass his days on artificial hills filled with peacocks. He never attempted to beseech women who showed unwillingness to share the bed with him for quarrels of love but wished that they, terrified at the muttering of clouds, would hide themselves in his breast. In autumnal nights he used to sport in a house adorned with a canopy and remove the toil of intercourse by enjoying the moon lustrous like a pearl. Through the windows of his palace he used to see the river Sarayu imitating the sports of his dear lady having the banks for her waist and the swans for the girdle. With closing eyes and the sound of girdles the youthful maidens used to attract Agnivarna. Casting their looks in the shape of feeble lights in an inner room divested of the wind the nights of the dewy season, just the proper season for the sexual intercourse, used to witness his sexual enjoyment. Beholding the mango leaves and blossoms dropped by the southern wind the women, making up differences, used to beseech Agnivarna stricken with their separation. He kept the women on his lap. And advising them to leave off the rope of the craddle he asked his servants to push it. And they, out of fear, used to clasp firmly his neck by their hands. Bedecked with evening decorations—*viz.*, sandal pastes on their breasts, robes thick set with pearls, and jewelled girdles the damsels used to serve him. With the drinking of the wine of Sahakara flowers their sexual desire, subdued with the end of the spring, was again excited. Thus desisting from the performance of other works and indulging in sensual pleasures at the excitement of Cupid Angivarna spent the seasons leaving marks on his limbs. His enemies, although they found him busy with pleasures, did not dare attack him on account of his great power. As the curse of the king Daksha influenced the moon so the dreadful disease of consumption, the outcome of excessive sexual indulgence, attacked him. He grew disobedient to the physicians and did not leave off the company of women and wine although he was aware of their evil effects. It is difficult to withdraw senses from their objects if they are once engaged in enjoying them. His countenance grew pale and he could not walk without any support. When the emperor was attacked with consumption the Raghu family looked like the sky with the last ray of the moon, a tank in summer with only mud left in it, and like a lamp with a feeble light. Keeping the disease of the king secret his courters announced to the subjects that the king was practising *Japa* in the day for procreating a son. Without seeing the face of a son who could keep up the continuity of the line although he had hundreds of wives the king could not bear the attack of the disease which was beyond the skill of the physicians like a lamp unable to bear the gust of a wind. Consulting with priests conversant in last rites his ministers brought his dead body into the garden attached to the Palace and threw it secretly into the burning fire. Then inviting speedily all the leading ladies of the palace they transferred the kingdom to the principal queen who showed evident signs of conception. He embryo was at first afflicted with hot tears begotten by the sorrow of separation from the king; but it was cooled down by the water sprinkled form golden pitchers. As the earth holds seeds sown in the month of Sravana, so she, holding the conception, for the well-being of the subjects who anxiously expected the hour of delivery, sat on the golden throne and governed the kingdom of her husband without any obstruction along with the hereditary aged ministers.

THE END.